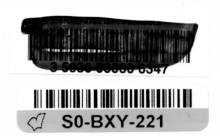

3 5936 00000 0347

S0-BXY-221

DATE DUE

DISCARD

DEMCO 38-296

Library I M C
Champaign Centennial High School
Champaign, Illinois

Modern Critical Interpretations

Fyodor Dostoevsky's
Crime and Punishment

Modern Critical Interpretations

The Oresteia
Beowulf
The General Prologue to
  The Canterbury Tales
The Pardoner's Tale
The Knight's Tale
The Divine Comedy
Exodus
Genesis
The Gospels
The Iliad
The Book of Job
Volpone
Doctor Faustus
The Revelation of St.
  John the Divine
The Song of Songs
Oedipus Rex
The Aeneid
The Duchess of Malfi
Antony and Cleopatra
As You Like It
Coriolanus
Hamlet
Henry IV, Part I
Henry IV, Part II
Henry V
Julius Caesar
King Lear
Macbeth
Measure for Measure
The Merchant of Venice
A Midsummer Night's
  Dream
Much Ado About
  Nothing
Othello
Richard II
Richard III
The Sonnets
Taming of the Shrew
The Tempest
Twelfth Night
The Winter's Tale
Emma
Mansfield Park
Pride and Prejudice
The Life of Samuel
  Johnson
Moll Flanders
Robinson Crusoe
Tom Jones
The Beggar's Opera
Gray's Elegy
Paradise Lost
The Rape of the Lock
Tristram Shandy
Gulliver's Travels

Evelina
The Marriage of Heaven
  and Hell
Songs of Innocence and
  Experience
Jane Eyre
Wuthering Heights
Don Juan
The Rime of the Ancient
  Mariner
Bleak House
David Copperfield
Hard Times
A Tale of Two Cities
Middlemarch
The Mill on the Floss
Jude the Obscure
The Mayor of
  Casterbridge
The Return of the Native
Tess of the D'Urbervilles
The Odes of Keats
Frankenstein
Vanity Fair
Barchester Towers
The Prelude
The Red Badge of
  Courage
The Scarlet Letter
The Ambassadors
Daisy Miller, The Turn
  of the Screw, and
  Other Tales
The Portrait of a Lady
Billy Budd, Benito Cer-
  eno, Bartleby the Scriv-
  ener, and Other Tales
Moby-Dick
The Tales of Poe
Walden
Adventures of
  Huckleberry Finn
The Life of Frederick
  Douglass
Heart of Darkness
Lord Jim
Nostromo
A Passage to India
Dubliners
A Portrait of the Artist as
  a Young Man
Ulysses
Kim
The Rainbow
Sons and Lovers
Women in Love
1984
Major Barbara

Man and Superman
Pygmalion
St. Joan
The Playboy of the
  Western World
The Importance of Being
  Earnest
Mrs. Dalloway
To the Lighthouse
My Antonia
An American Tragedy
Murder in the Cathedral
The Waste Land
Absalom, Absalom!
Light in August
Sanctuary
The Sound and the Fury
The Great Gatsby
A Farewell to Arms
The Sun Also Rises
Arrowsmith
Lolita
The Iceman Cometh
Long Day's Journey Into
  Night
The Grapes of Wrath
Miss Lonelyhearts
The Glass Menagerie
A Streetcar Named
  Desire
Their Eyes Were
  Watching God
Native Son
Waiting for Godot
Herzog
All My Sons
Death of a Salesman
Gravity's Rainbow
All the King's Men
The Left Hand of
  Darkness
The Brothers Karamazov
Crime and Punishment
Madame Bovary
The Interpretation of
  Dreams
The Castle
The Metamorphosis
The Trial
Man's Fate
The Magic Mountain
Montaigne's Essays
Remembrance of Things
  Past
The Red and the Black
Anna Karenina
War and Peace

These and other titles in preparation

Modern Critical Interpretations

Library I M C
Champaign Centennial High School
Champaign, Illinois

Fyodor Dostoevsky's
Crime and Punishment

Edited and with an introduction by

Harold Bloom
Sterling Professor of the Humanities
Yale University

Chelsea House Publishers
NEW YORK ◊ PHILADELPHIA

© 1988 by Chelsea House Publishers, a division
of Main Line Book Co.

Introduction © 1988 by Harold Bloom

All rights reserved. No part of this publication may be
reproduced or transmitted in any form or by any means
without the written permission of the publisher.

Printed and bound in the United States of America

10   9   8   7   6   5   4

∞ The paper used in this publication meets the minimum
requirements of the American National Standard for
Permanence of Paper for Printed Library Materials, Z39.48–
1984.

Library of Congress Cataloging-in-Publication Data
Fyodor Dostoevsky's Crime and punishment.
   (Modern critical interpretations)
   Bibliography: p.
   Includes index.
   Summary: Selected critical interpretations of
Dostoyevsky's novel "Crime and Punishment."
   1. Dostoyevsky, Fyodor, 1821–1881. Prestuplenie
i nakazanie. [1. Dostoyevsky, Fyodor, 1821–1881. Crime
and punishment. 2. Russian literature—History and
criticism] I. Bloom, Harold. II. Series.
PG3325.P73B55   1987   891.73'3   87-11799
ISBN 1-55546-066-6

Contents

Editor's Note

This book gathers together a representative selection of the best modern critical interpretations of Dostoevsky's novel, *Crime and Punishment*. The critical essays are reprinted here in the chronological order of their original publication. I am grateful to Joyce Banerjee and Henry Finder for their assistance in editing this volume.

My introduction centers upon Raskolnikov's quest for metaphysical freedom and power, a quest he does not so much repudiate as simply abandon. Alfred L. Bem begins the chronological sequence of criticism with a meditation upon the guilt-ridden consciousness of Raskolnikov. In Edward Wasiolek's reading, the poet W. D. Snodgrass's suggestion that the pawnbroker is a displaced representative of Raskolnikov's mother is expanded into a fuller psychoanalytic reading of the supposed displacement.

Michael Holquist investigates what he calls Raskolnikov's historicism as a clue to the puzzle of his motives. Raskolnikov's failure to repent, together with the extraordinary consciousness of Svidrigailov, is rightly seen by A. D. Nuttall as calling the Christian design of the novel into question. In Robert Louis Jackson's exegesis of part 1 of *Crime and Punishment*, the dialectics of consciousness operate so as to drive Raskolnikov "underground" towards murder, rather than to the desired goal of human love.

Derek Offord contextualizes the novel in the radical thought contemporary with Dostoevsky. Theory and life are seen as the true dialectical contraries of the novel by John Jones. Carnivalization, one of the great subjects of the celebrated Russian critic Mikhail Bakhtin, is related by him to the metaphor of space in *Crime and Punishment*, in a brief but highly evocative excursus that fittingly concludes this volume.

Introduction

Rereading *Crime and Punishment*, I am haunted suddenly by a recollection of my worst experience as a teacher. Back in 1955, an outcast instructor in the then New Critical, Neo-Christian Yale English department dominated by acolytes of the churchwardenly T. S. Eliot, I was compelled to teach *Crime and Punishment* in a freshman course to a motley collection of Yale legacies masquerading as students. Wearied of their response to Dostoevsky as so much more Eliotic Original Sin, I endeavored to cheer myself up (if not them) by reading aloud in class S. J. Perelman's sublime parody "A Farewell to Omsk," fragments of which are always with me, such as the highly Dostoevskian portrayal of the tobacconist Pyotr Pyotrvitch:

> "Good afternoon, Afya Afyakievitch!" replied the shop-keeper warmly. He was the son of a former notary public attached to the household of Prince Grashkin and gave himself no few airs in consequence. Whilst speaking it was his habit to extract a greasy barometer from his waistcoat and consult it importantly, a trick he had learned from the Prince's barber. On seeing Afya Afyakievitch he skipped about nimbly, dusted off the counter, gave one of his numerous offspring a box on the ear, drank a cup of tea, and on the whole behaved like a man of the world who has affairs of moment occupying him.

Unfortunately, my class did not think this funny and did not even enjoy the marvelous close of Perelman's sketch:

> "Don't take any flannel kopecks," said Afya gloomily. He dislodged a piece of horse-radish from his tie, shied it at a passing Nihilist, and slid forward into the fresh loam.

1

Dostoevsky had his own mode of humor, but he might not have appreciated Perelman either. *Crime and Punishment* is less apocalyptic than *The Brothers Karamazov,* but it is apocalyptic enough. It is also tendentious in the extreme, which is the point of Perelman's parody, but Dostoevsky is so great a tragedian that this does not matter. Raskolnikov is a powerful representation of the will demonized by its own strength, while Svidrigailov is beyond that, and stands on the border of a convincing phantasmagoria. Until the unfortunate epilogue, no other narrative fiction drives itself onwards with the remorseless strength of *Crime and Punishment,* truly a shot out of hell and into hell again. To have written a naturalistic novel that reads like a continuous nightmare is Dostoevsky's unique achievement.

Raskolnikov never does repent and change, unless we believe the epilogue, in which Dostoevsky himself scarcely believed. Despair causes his surrender to Porfiry, but even his despair never matches the fierce ecstasy he has achieved in violating all limits. He breaks what can be broken and yet does not break himself. He cannot be broken, not because he has found any truth, objective or psychological, but because he has known, however momentarily, the nihilistic abyss, a Gnostic freedom of what is beyond our sense of being creatures in God's creation. Konstantin Mochulsky is surely right to emphasize that Raskolnikov never comes to believe in redemption, never rejects his theory of strength and power. His surrender, as Mochulsky says, "is not a sign of penitence but of pusillanimity." We end up with a pre-Christian tragic hero ruined by blind fate, at least in his own vision. But this is about as unattractive as a tragic hero can be, because Raskolnikov comes too late in cultural history to seem a Prometheus rather than a bookish intellectual. In a Christian context, Prometheus assimilates to Satan, and Raskolnikov's pride begins to seem too satanic for tragedy.

Raskolnikov hardly persuades us on the level of Dostoevsky's Christian polemic, but psychologically he is fearsomely persuasive. Power for Raskolnikov can be defined as the ability to kill someone else, anyone at all, rather than oneself. I meet Raskolnikov daily, though generally not in so extreme a form, in many young contemporaries who constitute what I would call the School of Resentment. Their wounded narcissism, turned against the self, might make them poets or critics; turned outward, against others, it makes them eminent unrest-inducers. Raskolnikov does not move our sympathy *for him,* but he impresses us with his uncompromising intensity.

Svidrigailov may have been intended as Raskolnikov's foil, but he got

away from Dostoevsky, and runs off with the book, even as old Karamazov nearly steals the greater work away from the extraordinary Dmitri.
Raskolnikov is too pure a Promethean or devil to be interested in desire,
unless the object of desire be metaphysical freedom and power. He is a
kind of ascetic Gnostic, while Svidrigailov is a libertine Gnostic, attempting to liberate the sparks upward. If Raskolnikov portrays the madness of
the Promethean will, then Svidrigailov is beyond the will, as he is beyond
the still-religious affirmations of atheism. He lives (if that can be the right
word) a negativity that Raskolnikov is too much himself to attain. Raskolnikov killed for his own sake, he tells Sonia, to test his own strength. Svidrigailov is light years beyond that, on the way downwards and outwards
into the abyss, his foremother and forefather.

The best of all murder stories, *Crime and Punishment* seems to me beyond praise and beyond affection. Dostoevsky doubtless would impress
me even more than he does already if I could read Russian, but I would
not like him any better. A vicious obscurantism inheres in the four great
narratives, including *The Idiot* and *The Possessed,* and it darkens *Crime and
Punishment.* Only *The Brothers Karamazov* transcends Dostoevsky's hateful
ideology because the Karamazovs sweep past the truths that the novelist
continues to shout at us. Tolstoy did not think that Dostoevsky's final and
apocalyptic novel was one of the summits of the genre, but then he liked
to think of Dostoevsky as the Russian Harriet Beecher Stowe and would
have wanted old Karamazov to have resembled Simon Legree.

What seems to me strongest in Dostoevsky is the control of visionary
horror he shares with Blake, an imaginative prophet with whom he has
absolutely nothing else in common. No one who has read *Crime and
Punishment* ever can forget Raskolnikov's murder of poor Lizaveta:

> There in the middle of the floor, with a big bundle in her arms,
> stood Lizaveta, as white as a sheet, gazing in frozen horror at
> her murdered sister and apparently without the strength to cry
> out. When she saw him run in, she trembled like a leaf and her
> face twitched spasmodically; she raised her hand as if to cover
> her mouth, but no scream came and she backed slowly away
> from him towards the corner, with her eyes on him in a fixed
> stare, but still without a sound, as though she had no breath
> left to cry out. He flung himself forward with the axe; her lips
> writhed pitifully, like those of a young child when it is just be-
> ginning to be frightened and stands ready to scream, with its
> eyes fixed on the object of its fear. The wretched Lizaveta was

so simple, brow-beaten, and utterly terrified that she did not even put up her arms to protect her face, natural and almost inevitable as the gesture would have been at this moment when the axe was brandished immediately above it. She only raised her free left hand a little and slowly stretched it out towards him as though she were trying to push him away. The blow fell on her skull, splitting it open from the top of the forehead almost to the crown of the head, and felling her instantly. Raskolnikov, completely beside himself, snatched up her bundle, threw it down again, and ran to the entrance.

Nothing could be more painfully effective than: "She only raised her free left hand a little and slowly stretched it out towards him as though she were trying to push him away." We think of the horrible dream in which Raskolnikov sees a poor, lean, old mare beaten to death with a crowbar, and we may reflect upon Nietzsche's darkest insights: that pain creates memory, so that the pain is the meaning, and meaning is therefore painful. Dostoevsky was a great visionary and an exuberant storyteller, but there is something paradoxically nihilistic in his narrative visions. The sublime mode asks us to give up easier pleasures for more difficult pleasures, which is altogether an aesthetic request. Dostoevsky belongs not to the sublime genre but to the harsher perspectives of the apocalyptic. He insists that we accept pains that transcend aesthetic limits. His authority at apocalypse is beyond question, but such authority also has its own aesthetic limits.

The Problem of Guilt

Alfred L. Bem

It is often said that Dostoevsky's "novel-tragedy" gravitates toward a single major "catastrophic" event, one usually connected with a crime; what has not been sufficiently stressed is that Dostoevsky's focus is not crime at all, but its corollary—guilt. . . . We shall not be concerned here with any objective norms of guilt and crime, but only with those psychological substrata on which these norms rest. . . . Crime will be understood only as the *awareness by the subject himself of some moral norm which he has violated,* quite apart from whether this violation has been recognized externally, morally, as a real crime. Without such a limitation [in the definition of crime] the correlation between guilt and crime, which plays such a crucial role in Dostoevsky, would be incomprehensible. Quite often, particularly in Dostoevsky's earlier works, the feeling of guilt becomes extremely and even tragically intense when only an extremely vague sense of a concrete crime lends support to this feeling. In other words, the objective crime which awakens a feeling of guilt may turn out to be so insignificant as to provide no explanation for the intense feeling of guilt. In this case the tragedy of guilt can be understood and disclosed only by presupposing that the *concrete crime serves as a surrogate for some crime not openly manifested yet present in the psyche,* like a trauma or pressure of conscience.

To understand Dostoevsky's thought one must allow for the presence in the human psyche of a feeling of sinfulness as such, independent of the existence of any concrete crime—what we might call *the feeling of original*

From *Twentieth-Century Interpretations of* Crime and Punishment, edited by Robert Louis Jackson. © 1974 by Prentice-Hall, Inc.

sin. . . . We can assume, then, that the feeling of sin, of guilt can be present in the psyche unaccompanied by any consciousness of crime. Indeed, the guilt-ridden consciousness often seeks a crime, as though it wished to free itself from an overwhelming sense of fatality and enter the world of ordinary human criminality, apparently more tolerable to human consciousness than the intense pressure of metaphysical sinfulness. It is only here that we can find an explanation for Dostoevsky's idea that "each of us is guilty for all," and for his characteristic notion of the "desire to suffer." With the latter in mind we can turn to the episode in *Crime and Punishment* with the house painter Mikolka, the workman who takes on himself Raskolnikov's crime. The episode is a minor one, but of central importance for our theme.

No one first meeting the painter Mikolka Dementiev suspected in him a spiritual complexity which would lead to his puzzing assumption of guilt for the murder of the old lady. We find an ingenuous, life-loving lad, with a taste for the bottle. Porfiry Petrovich, a man not without insight, characterizes him this way:

> First he's immature, still a child; and not that he's a coward, but sensitive, a kind of artist type. Yes, really. You mustn't laugh at me for explaining him like that. He is innocent and completely impressionable. He has feelings; he is a fantast. He can sing and dance, and they say he can tell stories so people gather from all around to listen. And he'll go to school and he'll laugh himself silly because somebody somehow crooked a finger at him; and he'll drink himself senseless, not because he's a drunkard, but just every now and then, when people buy him drinks; he's like a child still.
>
> (part 6, chap. 2)

This characterization tallies completely with our first impression of the house painters on the day of the murder. The witnesses unanimously testified that there was nothing suspicious in their conduct. Both painters, Nikolai and Dmitri, ran out of the courtyard and began to pummel each other in fun. . . . How is it possible that this apparently simple person could come to take on himself somebody else's crime? This psychological enigma must be solved, and Dostoevsky does so; but as usual when a psychological explanation is to be found in the unconscious, Dostoevsky provides an explanation on a conscious level: in this case, introducing the motif of "fear" that he, Mikolka, would be convicted. This fear overcomes Mikolka when he learns about the murder of the old lady and feels guilty because he had picked up the earrings dropped by the murderer; his fear of being accused became unbearable and he wants to hang himself. Dostoevsky tries to give the reader a convincing explanation of Mikolka's behavior by making us aware of Mikolka's internal distress; but he does not yet make it clear to us why Mikolka decided to assume somebody else's guilt. Porfiry Petrovich hints at the reason for this strange behavior; he suggests that the explanation must be sought elsewhere in Mikolka's moral experiences. The house painter turns out not to be so spiritually uncomplicated as we had imagined; he has his own enigmatic past. Porfiry Petrovich observes:

> But did you know that he was a Raskolnik [schismatic, sectarian—ED.]? Well, not a Raskolnik, exactly, but a member of one of those religious sects. There were members of his family who were Runners; they'd run away from worldly involvement. He himself actually spent two years, not long ago, under the spiritual tutelage of some holy elder in some village. . . . He himself was moved to run off into the wilderness! He had the spirit, would pray to God at night, read the old "true" books and reread them, for hours on end. . . . Well, now, in jail it seems he remembered the honorable elder, and the Bible turned up again, too. Do you know what they mean, Rodion Romanych, when they talk of "taking suffering upon themselves"? They don't mean suffering for anybody in particular, just "one has to suffer." That means, *accept* suffering; and if it's from the authorities, so much the better. . . . You mean you won't admit that our people produce fantastic characters of this sort? Yes, many. Now the elder is beginning to have some effect again, especially after that business with the noose.
>
> (part 6, chap. 2)

The way was clearly prepared for Mikolka's "fantastic" behavior. The news of the murder which had so disconcerted him and led him to attempt suicide was only the most immediate cause which brought to the surface those feelings of guilt that were hidden in the depths of his unconscious.

Precisely the problem of guilt lay at the root of Mikolka's act, not a superficial "fear" of conviction; indeed, Dostoevsky originally had no intention at all of introducing the latter motive. Twice in the notebooks to the novel he stresses the basic "religious" motive in Mikolka's behavior. Thus, in one part of the manuscript we read: "A workman testifies against himself (he had got caught up with religion), wanted to suffer (but gets muddled). They start pressuring him. And an old man sits there: one has to suffer, he says." A brief note appears in another place. "News at the gathering that a man (a workman) was taken by religion."

We can see from these notes that the root of Mikolka's behavior lay in a "religious" feeling linked with his moral experiences. The fact that Dostoevsky associates these elements in Mikolka's consciousness with the influences of some old religious sectarian serving a prison term with him testifies to Dostoevsky's artistic awareness. Such views on the primordial sinfulness of man were widespread in Russian sectarian religious thought.

One might suspect Dostoevsky of using the whole Mikolka episode only as an artful manoeuvre in the development of a detective story, a way of mixing the cards and holding back the denouement. But his supreme artistry is revealed in another way: concerned with narrative technique, he nevertheless introduces instead of a shallow plot device an incident which is closely connected with the central idea of the novel—the problem of guilt. The house painter, in contradistinction to Raskolnikov who strives to evade responsibility before his conscience for his sin, assumes responsibility for a crime that he did not commit. The interplay between these two responses to the problem of guilt will become even clearer after we examine Raskolnikov's crime.

Mikolka, according to Dostoevsky, "got caught up with religion" under the influence of an old religious sectarian; but in order to get caught up on religion he must have had some spiritual motivation. We must therefore assume a feeling of general sinfulness, of primordial guilt in the depths of Mikolka's consciousness, or, more accurately, in his unconscious—a feeling which sought expression in taking suffering upon himself. The "desire to suffer" cannot be explained without the supposition that there is a primordial feeling of guilt, the experience of primordial sinfulness, at the basis of the human soul. The incident involving Mikolka in *Crime and Punishment* is only an artistic expression of this phenomenon observed by Dostoevsky in the depths of his own being. . . .

Raskolnikov, a prisoner of his idée fixe, kills an old money lender. The whole novel is built around the unique process of disintegration in the hero's soul: his intellectual life is split off from the life of feeling. I do not know how I can express my thought more precisely here. A state of spiritual unity and harmony gives way to a "disintegration" in which one aspect of a person's being becomes overextended and eclipses the rest. But though driven into the unconscious these other aspects of self can remain active there and affect conduct in a special way. It is still possible then, paradoxically, for a criminal in his acts to preserve some inner nobility: just this inner split in Raskolnikov is the content of *Crime and Punishment*.

Crime is presented here as an unquestioned fact, not only in the formal but also the moral sense. But this fact does not penetrate Raskolnikov's consciousness; it takes the form in his unconscious of a potential power of conscience. To the very end, mind remains unrepentant. Even in prison, after his conviction, Raskolnikov still holds inflexibly to the idea that the murder is justifiable. And yet his whole being, his entire moral nature is shaken precisely by the moral aspect of the murder. Like a shadow, Sonia continually follows him and directs him onto the path of repentance. Dostoevsky portrays this symbolic role of Sonia with amazing power. When Raskolnikov wavers in his decision to confess, Sonia at that very moment is with him as his embodied conscience. As he leaves the police station he sees her:

> There, not far from the gate, stood Sonia, numb and deathly pale; and she looked at him with a wild look. He stopped before her. There was something painful and tortured in her face, something desperate. She threw up her hands. A ghastly, lost smile forced its way to his lips. He stood there and grinned. Then he turned back upstairs to the station.
>
> (part 6, chap. 8)

His fate is decided: he confesses to killing the old woman.

Here, then, is an extraordinary situation: in the absence of any conscious feeling, guilt is not only subconsciously present but even determines the final outcome of the spiritual drama. Thus, Dostoevsky is right when he envisages the possibility, too, of Raskolnikov's spiritual resurrection, that is, the restoration of his spiritual unity.

Raskolnikov's Motives: Love and Murder

Edward Wasiolek

W. D. Snodgrass's reading of *Crime and Punishment* brought into the center of attention a whole part of the novel that had largely been ignored by the "classic" explanations of Raskolnikov's motives. He was the first to perceive the tangled and bruising relations between Raskolnikov and his mother, and the first to perceive that the landlady and the pawnbroker are displaced representations of Raskolnikov's mother, so that in striking at the pawnbroker Raskolnikov was striking symbolically at the mother. Before Snodgrass's article was published, very little had been said about the relations between mother and son, and almost nothing about the part these relations play in the murder of the pawnbroker, even though one-fourth of the novel concerns Raskolnikov's relations with his mother.

The sections dealing with Raskolnikov and his mother show hidden aggression toward each other. The mother is intent on reminding Raskolnikov how much she and Dunia have sacrificed for him and how much they are willing to sacrifice for him. Although the mother dwells on her love and affection, she reminds him subtly of his subjecting them to misery and hardship through his refusal to continue his studies and to support himself at the university. Raskolnikov in turn has passively and intentionally revolted against the burden of his mother's love and sacrifice by defeating her expectations of success. He gives up his studies, refuses to find work, and permits himself to fall into dependence and degradation.

The punishing relations between mother and son may not be immedi-

From *American Imago* 31, no. 3 (Fall 1974). © 1974 by the Association for Applied Psychoanalysis, Inc.

ately perceptible, but the powerful emotional ties between them and between brother and sister are clearly visible in a number of scenes. When Raskolnikov receives the letter from his mother in part 1, chapter 3, his hands tremble; he is visibly perturbed during the reading; and then rushes out of his room in a half-demented state. When he first sees his mother and sister in the narrative time of the story, he faints, a psychic defense against the painful reality of their presence.

Snodgrass's analogy between the mother and the pawnbroker implies that Raskolnikov has a murderous hostility toward his mother. Raskolnikov himself tells us that he hates his mother and sister: Near the end of part 3, he says to himself: "Mother, sister—how I loved them! Why do I hate them now? Yes, I hate them, I feel physical hatred for them. I can't bear them near me." Snodgrass supports the tie between mother, landlady and pawnbroker by pointing out that each is a widow, each is accompanied by a younger woman (Dunia, Natalya, and Lizaveta), that Raskolnikov places himself in a position of indebtedness to each of the women, and that Raskolnikov has fantasies of violence against each. Snodgrass summarizes the resemblance between the three women: "For if Raskolnikov has intentionally picked Alyona Ivanovna to stand in the image of Pashenka, he has picked both to stand in the image of his mother. They form a triumvirate of older women, each accompanied by a younger woman, each a widow. From each, Raskolnikov has asked and received something; to each he is indebted. They hold his spirit as a pledge. They seem to him tormentors, since it is on their account that he torments himself. When Raskolnikov strikes down the pawnbroker with an axe, he will strike at Pashenka, but he will also strike behind her at the image of his greatest creditor, his mother." Snodgrass might also have pointed out what may be the most telling evidence of all in connecting the pawnbroker and the mother. Near the end of part 3 and following the passage in which Raskolnikov expresses his hate for his mother and sister, he slips imperceptibly in his reflections from talking about hating his mother to talking about hating the "old woman." He says, "Ah, how I hate the old woman now! I feel I should kill her again if she came to life!" The shift from mother to pawnbroker is evidence of how they are associated in his mind; even more significant: it is not possible to establish from the word "old woman" which woman he is referring to. It is in all probability an intentional ambiguity.

Snodgrass's brilliant perception of the similarities between the three women is, I believe, established convincingly. There are a number of other points of similarity which Snodgrass does not mention and to which I will come later on. The most pressing question, however, is why Raskolnikov felt such murderous rage against his mother and why he had to expend such hate in a displaced and disguised way. The answer lies partly in the social, religious, and ethical prohibitions of a society that inhibits one's expression of hostility toward a loved one, especially against a parent. But, it is not merely a matter of external checks. The child finds it painful to permit himself the conscious thought, let alone an action of violence against a parent. Since the hate, by the law of psychic economy, has to go somewhere, it will tend to be displaced on someone else chosen as a surrogate for the loved one or, as is also quite frequent, it will be expended against oneself. The more violent the hate and the closer the loved one, the more hidden and more remote will be the object against which the hate will be expended. Such remote expressions are necessary to protect Raskolnikov against the pain of directly expressed hostility.

The same kind of veiling can be observed in regard to his sister and his relationship to the landlady's daughter and to Lizaveta. Such concealment can be explained by the need to protect himself against a conscious admission of erotic affection for his sister. Dunia, like her mother, is a strikingly handsome girl, robust in body, intelligence, and temperament. The landlady's daughter is sickly, passive, and mentally somewhat undeveloped. The pawnbroker's sister is even less attractive physically and less developed mentally: she is ungainly, a half-wit, and she passively endures the outrages of the older sister and the sexual aggressions of various men. It is significant that the disguises progress toward overtness of sexuality, since Raskolnikov "loves" the landlady's daughter in a compassionate and spiritual sense, but the pawnbroker's sister is repeatedly and coarsely seduced by other men.

By and large, the displacements both of mother and sister are constructed to move toward an overt expression of what is hidden. Such progression can be discerned to control a number of traits. Raskolnikov is indebted, for example, to each of the women and there is a progression toward active manipulation by him of that indebtedness, that is, toward a revelation of his part in "choosing" the indebtedness and consequently of progression toward the consciousness of what he is doing. His indebtedness to his mother seems at first to be the result of untoward circumstances; but on closer examination, it is possible to see Raskolnikov's passive part in contracting the indebtedness. His role in arranging his indebtedness to the landlady and then blaming her for punishing him, comes out quite clearly when, later in the novel, we hear Razumikhin's version of the facts. As for his indebtedness to the pawnbroker, he actively and openly arranges to make himself the indebtor and her the debtor. The same progression from the hidden to something open can be seen in the physical traits of the three women. The mother is a strikingly beautiful woman (her name Pulkheriya means beautiful), the landlady is in Raskolnikov's eyes unattractive (although we learn later from Razumikhin that she is quite attractive), and the pawnbroker is ugly and hateful. He feels oppressed and tormented by his mother, but carefully refrains from expressing to himself what he feels; he feels tormented by his landlady and says so; and he goes out of his way to dwell on the hateful and tormenting qualities of the pawnbroker. We go from hidden hate to overt hate, as we go from mother, to landlady, to pawnbroker. The point of such a progression is an indication of the disguises that Raskolnikov must go through before he will permit the hate and hostility to rise in his consciousness. Snodgrass failed to point out the progressions, but they support his basic identifications.

It is clear that Snodgrass is acquainted with psychoanalytic concepts, even though he never mentions Freud or psychoanalysis or uses any technical terms. Such basic concepts as displacement, defenses, reaction formation, projection, introjection and internalized aggression lie just below the surface of his argument and his conclusions. There is the possibility that he did not choose to name them or use them more explicitly to avoid the automatic and uncritical negative reactions that such terms and methods often arouse in literary audiences. More probably, his psychoanalytic knowledge came not so much from explicit acquaintance as from the general diffusion of Freudian concepts in our culture. The latter surmise is supported by the fact that he never mentions Freud in the long article, but does mention Edmund Bergler and Simone Weil. Bergler would have taken him to Freud, and Weil away from Freud and to the generalized philosophical and religious conclusions which finally neutralize, and in my opinion, distort, his psychoanalytic perceptions.

It is not Snodgrass's reluctance to use psychoanalytic terms that I have reservations about, but his failure to make the most of his excellent analogy by the use of systematic psychoanalytic thinking. This failure led him to miss that opposites like beauty and ugliness (mother and pawnbroker) and moral robustness and frailty (sister and pawnbroker's sister) can also be similarities. It also led him to miss the supporting progressions, which the psychoanalytic processes of displacement of painful experiences on to increasingly remote surrogates. In the course of the article, Snodgrass veers from the psychoanalytic implications of his analogy to vaguely social-moralistic conclusions. This shift is particularly perceptible in Snod-grass's explanation of Raskolnikov's motives toward which the entire arti-cle moves. The groundwork is laid for a new and different explanation of Raskolnikov's motives; yet the conclusions that are drawn from psychoan-alytic perceptions bring his argument back to familiar and inadequate social-moralitic explanations.

Snodgrass himself summarizes his four-part explanation of Raskolni-kov's motives at the beginning of the article as "the desire to achieve pun-ishment which will reinstate him as a worthy member of a moral uni-verse." Such an explanation may be true on a moral and philosophical level, but Raskolnikov's drama is not only a philosophical treatise but also a painful, torturing personal drama. Snodgrass's conclusions do not ex-plain adequately what the experience means to Raskolnikov, and don't do justice to his own perceptive analogy between mother and pawnbroker. Raskolnikov's personal drama has to do with the hostility he suffers and provokes in regard to his mother, and the symbolic attempt to resolve the hostility by striking out against the mother. There is a hiatus between Snodgrass's perceptions and his conclusions. Much of the article has to do with Raskolnikov's relations with his mother, but the conclusions are re-stricted to a social and religious context.

It is true that Raskolnikov attempts to do with society what he has done with his mother, to implicate it in his suffering, to raise in his con-sciousness a conception of society which aggresses against him, so that he may be justified in striking out against it. He tells Sonia more than once, as he tells Dunia near the end of the novel, that he has done nothing more in murdering the pawnbroker than society does as a matter of course. He pursues the punishment of society so that he can feel victimized, and thus justified; and on a deeper level, so that by the punishment he may be, as Snodgrass suggests, forced back into the fold of humanity. The same drama can be seen as pursuit of punishment for religious ends, or at least Sonia raises it to this level. He aggresses against God, so that God will show the limits of freedom and moral law. Without raising the question of relative importance, I would maintain that the personal drama comes before the social and religious dramas. The grudge that is elevated into ag-gression against society and God is first a grudge and aggression against his loved ones, and it is Snodgrass's reading that has permitted us to glimpse what the sources of that grudge may be. His feelings run high againt the society that has "degraded" him, but his feelings run deeper against the family he feels has degraded him.

Snodgrass's translations of the personal drama into social and religious terms can be seen in his reading of the mare-beating dream. His conclusion about the dream is the following:

> The dream shows Raskolnikov to himself as a man too feeble in drawing his burdens, yet entirely too strong in punishing himself for that failure. Thus he is stuck on a treadmill of guilt and rage where he is beating himself to death for being stuck. At the same time, the dream shows him a world which has the same characteristics: all good characters are weak or victimized. (The dream contains but disguises the fact that these characters have chosen to be either weak or victimized.) Meantime, "the worst are full of passionate intensity." The only active role in the dream belongs to such destroyers as Mikolka. Raskolnikov's drama tells him that he must choose either murder or suicide, either kill or be killed.

The interpretation assumes that we can make a neat distinction in the dream between the victimized and the victimizers. Yet this is not so, even by the identifications that Snodgrass himself gives us. He perceives correctly that the mare (the victimized creature in the dream) stands not only for the teen-age girl on the boulevard, (Dunia, Sonia, Marmeladov), and the mother, but also for Raskolnikov and the pawnbroker. He sees also that the pawnbroker is to be identified with Mikolka (the victimizers and the destroyers), but he does not see, or at least does not mention, that the mother, the landlady, Dunia, and Marmeladov can also be identified with the destroyers and the victimizers. Much of Snodgrass's article, after all, shows us how artfully his mother, and to a lesser extent his sister, have victimized Raskolnikov, and how by analogy Marmeladov has, through his passive actions, victimized his daughter Sonia and his wife Katerina. If Raskolnikov, the pawnbroker, the mother, the sister, and Marmeladov are both Mikolka and the mare, both victimizers and victimized, how can we come to the conclusion that the dream shows Raskolnikov that he "must choose either murder or suicide, either kill or be killed"? Who are the murderers and who are the victims? Snodgrass sees also that Raskolnikov comprises all the actors in the dream, but he fails to see that this is evidence against his conclusions that the drama shows us a Raskolnikov who must choose between a world in which one is victimized or one in which one is the victimizer. In order for Raskolnikov to have a choice between victim and victimizer, between suicide and murder, Raskolnikov must be able to separate himself from what is being represented. The dream does not show us, as Snodgrass suggests, Raskolnikov and a state of things outside of Raskolnikov. The choices have already been made and the dream shows us what they are. The pawnbroker, landlady, Sonia, Dunia, Lizaveta, Marmeladov, Katerina have the meaning Raskolnikov assigns to them.

What Snodgrass has done is "rationalize" the dream, giving it a general character of an intellectualist sort. What the dream actually shows us—and we must always remember that it is Raskolnikov's dream—is Raskolnikov killing his mother, the pawnbroker, and the landlady, and in turn being tormented and killed by them. Most of all, it shows us a Raskolnikov who is killing himself, who is tormentor and tormented, victimizer and victimized, killer and being killed. Since it is he who assigns the roles to the mother, landlady, pawnbroker, they exist as meanings within him; they are what he has decided them to be. In killing them, he attempts to kill what they mean in him, and what they mean to him is that they are his tormentors and victimizers. But in striking at them, he strikes at himself. If they are his tormentors, he does not silence the tormenting by tormenting, but only increases it because he is both tormentor and tormented. The dream shows us that the ferocity of hostility against his real or imagined tormentors is also directed against himself. We are shown no contemplative Raskolnikov in the dream observing a state of things that asks him to choose between murder and suicide. The dream gives him no choice at all, but it does dramatize the futility of doing both; the blow against others is struck against himself. Raskolnikov will tell us later the same thing: that in killing the old hag, he had killed himself, and the symbolic reenactment of the killing of the pawnbroker, at the end of part 3, tells us again that he had not been able to kill the pawnbroker within himself, even though she has "actually" been killed. What he had not been able to kill is the pawnbroker within him.

Still, if I am correct in stating that the dream shows us that Raskolnikov, in striking at others, is striking at himself and that the punishment of the tormentors is a punishment of himself, I will have corrected Snodgrass's interpretation of the dream, but I will not have met the objections I brought forth to his social-religious conclusions. Snodgrass tell us that Raskolnikov desires punishment for the deep sense of shame and wrong he feels within himself, but he does not tell us what that shame and wrong are. I have indicated that Raskolnikov has attempted to punish his tormentors, and has succeeded only in punishing himself, but I have not explained why he feels he must punish his tormentors with such ferocity and why Dostoevsky felt it necessary to translate the punishment into self-punish-

Library I M C
Champaign Centennial High School
Champaign, Illinois

ment. Why does Raskolnikov feel that he must kill the pawnbroker and through her symbolically the mother? What moves him to pursue punishment and self-punishment with such relentless and undeviating ferocity? What is it that has persuaded him that the experiment will be a failure before it has begun, so that it is not really an experiment but only a confirmation? And a confirmation of what?

II

Near the end of the novel Raskolnikov says to Dunia: "Oh, if only I were alone and no one loved me and I too had never loved anyone! Nothing of all this would have happened." This is a tantalizing and mysterious statement, made after the crime and the agony and somewhat in the cold reflection of everything that had happened. If we take this statement literally, Raskolnikov is saying that "love" caused everything: the guilt, the search for punishment and the attempt to alleviate the guilt by murdering the pawnbroker and symbolically the murder of the mother. If we turn to his relationship to his loved ones—his mother and sister—we find ample evidence that his love for them and theirs for him are entwined with a great deal of hostility and aggression. It is their sacrificial love that drives him to the half-demented fury with which he leaves his little room and rushes out into the street muttering to himself; it is this same sacrificial love that causes him to throw Luzhin out of his room without a provocation that is commensurate with the ferocity of Raskolnikov's reactions. It is their presence that causes him to faint, that provokes him to express hatred for them, and that leads him to flaunt his relationship with Sonia before his mother. We can explain his reactions by saying that he feels victimized by the sacrificial love of mother and sister, for such love predetermines what he will be and what he must be, just as Marmeladov is victimized by Katerina by her insistence that he be like her imagined first husband. Marmeladov is permitted only the identity that Katerina Ivanovna will give him: the dutiful, sober husband who resembles her first husband, or at least as she imagines him to have been. Raskolnikov is permitted only the identity that mother and sister give him: the dutiful son, hard-working, morally undeviating, and destined to bring security and honor to them. Marmeladov tells Katerina by his destructive actions that she must accept him as he is and not as she thinks he ought to be. Since she refuses to relinquish the Marmeladov she has formed in her mind, he destroys the image by acting out another Marmeladov. His destructive acts are both aggression and appeal. The aggression is against the Marmeladov she insists he must be, and his appeal is to be accepted for what he really is. Something of the same aggression and appeal can be seen in Raskolnikov's relations with his mother. It is as if Raskolnikov were saying to his mother: I am not what you think I am, I am even the very opposite. I am not the ideal son, I am secretly the hateful son. You have the ideal image, but I am the vicious reality. Indeed, he says this in almost the same words in the notebooks.

Raskolnikov's revolt against the burden of his sister's and mother's love and against the constraint of his freedom, implied by their expectations, gives us what would seem to be an adequate explanation of his furious actions. Such an explanation would justify the subplot of the Marmeladovs and even more important would explain why it is necessary to strike out symbolically against the mother in killing the pawnbroker. But the explanation is wrong, or at least inadequate, because it assumes that the sacrificial love is a cause, when it is really an effect. The burdensome sacrificial love is something that Raskolnikov has chosen, not something that has driven him to other choices. He *chooses* to drop out of school, to be poor, to lie for days with an empty stomach in his coffin-like room; in short, he chooses the very conditions that provoke his mother to sacrifice and Dunia to become a governess at the Svidrigaylovs, to suffer near rape and disgrace, and then to choose legal prostitution with Luzhin. And if he chooses the sacrificial love, the love cannot be the cause of his agony and his guilt. The situation is complicated, of course, and not as schematic as I have put it, for both theory and the actual narrative line of the novel show that there is an interaction between Raskolnikov's provoking his family to sacrifice and his suffering from such sacrifice; but, whatever the part that the choice plays—and it plays some part—it is clear that something other than the burdensome sacrificial love moves him to the murder.

In attempting to get at this something other, we cannot overlook the dense web of erotic relations that exist in the novel. Psychoanalysis will lead us, of course, to some erotic relationship against which the individual will protect himself in various ways. One such way is to intellectualize and consequently impersonalize the painful content. It cannot escape our attention that Raskolnikov's overt motivations: to be a benefactor of family and humanity or to be a superman exempt from the normal constraints of law are such intellectualizings and impersonalizations. Raskolnikov seems to be saying: I did the murder because I am a special and heroic personality. Such a possibility is substantiated by the frequent outbursts of abuse against himself.

In attempting to get at the explanation of why Raskolnikov should feel himself to be hateful, I have no intention of reducing the complexities and refinements of Raskolnikov's drama to an oedipal complex. I have too much respect for literature to make it—and especially this novel—an example of static and abstract psychoanalytic generalizations. Nor do I think that psychoanalysis—when applied to life or to literature—leads one to such crude oversimplifications. If I can add to Belinsky's dictum "Life is higher than art," I would say that literature is "higher" than psychoanalysis or indeed any set of propositions that we frame to explain life or literature. Freud and psychoanalysis, however, have added immensely to our store of hypothetical generalizations about psychology; and since psychology is inevitably part of literature, it would seem both rational and academic to take such propositions into consideration.

Dostoevsky lived in a society which repressed direct sexual expression, and his difficulties with editors in using even the mildest of sexual terms are evidence that the taboos were strictly enforced. Yet, it is remarkable how much of a sexual nature he expressed in the novel, although necessarily in disguised and oblique form. Snodgrass touches on sexual implications of the murder in a few casual remarks, such as the spasm that Raskolnikov experiences as he fumbles with the keys and attempts to open the old hag's trunk. But he quickly translates the sexual content into metaphors for Raskolnikov's self-abuse: "Yet, because of Raskolnikov's deep identification with Alyona Ivanovna, the murder must finally be seen not as an act of sexual violence directed against another; but rather as an act of self-destruction and 'self-abuse.'" But the image of Raskolnikov rummaging under the old woman's bed, and below the clothes in the trunk to get at her "treasure," (a word that is used in colloquial Russian for a woman's sexual favors) should not be ignored. Less obvious but perhaps more significant, the aggression of mother against son and son against mother is played out not only on economic and career levels, but also on a sexual level. Raskolnikov's choice of women he falls in love with is calculated to give hurt to his mother and to provoke her aggression against them. We are told that Madame Raskolnikov so disapproved of his choice of the landlady's daughter that she was happy when the girl died. Similarly, she disapproves of Sonia and is convinced that Sonia is at the bottom of all their misfortunes. In a scene, reminiscent of Hamlet's behavior at the dumb show when Hamlet aggresses against his mother by choosing to lay his head on Ophelia's lap and to talk to her in coarse sexual terms (instead of responding to his mother's invitation to sit next to her), Raskolnikov insists on inviting Sonia, when she comes to invite him to the funeral dinner, to enter his room and sit in the presence of his mother, to the mother's obvious discomfort and disapproval.

There is evidence, also, of an erotic relationship with his sister. Raskolnikov has chosen women to fall in love with who would least remind him of his sister. Dunia is robust in body and mind, and the landlady's daughter is weak in both. Dunia is firm and willful, Sonia is timid and self-effacing. There is no expressed antagonism on the part of Dunia toward Sonia in the novel, but such antagonism is expressed in the notebooks: "The sister becomes Sonia's worst enemy; she sets Razumikhin against her; gets him to insult her; and afterward when Razumikhin goes over to Sonia's side, she quarrels with him." There are too, on several occasions, signs of embarrassed and ambiguous affection between brother and sister. But perhaps the most telling evidence for such a suppressed erotic relationship is to be seen in Raskolnikov's behavior toward Dunia's two suitors. The gratuitous rage Raskolnikov feels against Luzhin bespeaks of feelings that are pent up, barely restrained, and powerful enough to break through the politeness and courtesy of social intercourse. Raskolnikov's feelings against the actual attempted seducer of Dunia, Svidrigaylov, are less intense. To be sure, he warns Svidrigaylov to stay away from his sister, but he does this in a relatively calm and rational way. There are no unreasoned and uncontained outbursts against Svidrigaylov, even when the latter describes in detail how he attempted to seduce Raskolnikov's sister. Indeed, when Svidrigaylov tells how he attempted to seduce Dunia, and how there was a point in which she seemed to be giving in, Raskolnikov listens to the long narrative without interrupting Svidrigaylov. We can only conclude—given his propensity to break out emotionally on many other scores—that he listens with rapt attention and enjoys the narrative vicariously. How does one explain the viciousness of his response to Dunia's legal fiancé and the mildness of his response to Svidrigaylov's dishonorable advances? One explanation would be that Svidrigaylov had been repulsed by Dunia and is therefore not an imminent threat to whatever erotic feelings he has for his sister, whereas at the time of his violent outburst against Luzhin, Luzhin was the legal fiancé and seemed to be on his way to obtain legally what Svidrigaylov had failed to do directly. But there is another explanation. If we are to take Dostoevsky's words in the notebooks literally that Svidrigaylov is supposed to represent one side of Raskolnikov and that Svidrigaylov is an overt expression of what is unexpressed in Raskolnikov, then it would seem that we would have to look at Svidrigaylov's sexual aggressiveness as in some way an externalization of what is hidden in Raskolnikov's unconscious.

Critics (myself included) have taken Dostoevsky's words as justification for seeing Svidrigaylov as a philosophic embodiment of Raskolnikov's desire to be above morality. Svidrigaylov is the bronze man Raskolnikov had hoped to become by the murder. If we can use Svidrigaylov as a symbolic equivalent for hidden philosophical and moral motives in Raskolnikov, then we cannot deny them as symbolic equivalents for other motives, among which the erotic motives loom large. Svidrigaylov has murdered, as Raskolnikov has murdered; he whips his servant and his wife, as Raskolnikov symbolically whips the landlady, and as he beats his mother and sister in the notebooks. Svidrigaylov is indebted to his wife, as Raskolnikov contrives to indebt himself to the landlady, pawnbroker and mother. Svidrigaylov has violated and apparently caused the death of a young girl, and has on at least two occasions attempted to violate Raskolnikov's sister. Raskolnikov may be repelled by the dirt Svidrigaylov has surrounded himself with, but he is also attracted to it, as the meeting between them in the tavern makes abundantly clear. Svidrigaylov understands this and regales Raskolnikov with stories of his sexual exploits in a manner of complicity.

But it is not only Svidrigaylov who represents the hidden impulses of Raskolnikov, but also Sonia. Again both the notebooks and the structure of the novel are explicit on this point. If we can use Svidrigaylov as a dramatic externalization of hidden sexual motives in Raskolnikov, it would seem that Sonia cannot by any stretch of the critical imagination find a place in such an explanation. Dostoevsky himself in the notebooks indicated that they should be taken as opposite externalizations of Raskolnikov, and the dominant critical tradition has seen Raskolnikov as torn between his "Sonia principle" and his "Svidrigaylov principle." I believe this interpretation to be correct, but again they are opposites on more than philosophical and moral grounds. We must remind ourselves that Sonia is a prostitute, and it is only to her, a prostitute, that he is ineluctably drawn. What Raskolnikov cannot get over is that Sonia is a prostitute but is unsullied, and remains pure. What fascinates him is her "clean-dirtiness." She represents for him a resolution of what is clean and what is dirty; she redeems in his eyes the dirty life she has been forced to lead, and it is this redemptive quality that attracts him to her.

I am aware that it may go against our aesthetic sense to think of Sonia in sexual terms, especially in view of the fact that she has been discussed almost exclusively in spiritual terms. But she is a prostitute, and is looked upon by Lebeziatnikov and the Marmeladovs' landlady as morally unfit to live in the apartment house. Since Raskolnikov's erotic feelings for his mother are deeply repressed and highly displaced, one would expect that they would be permitted expression only under the most exceptional circumstances and would be projected on someone who would not arouse erotic feelings. Sonia is such a person: her sexuality is barely perceptible and disguised by the unquestioned spirituality of her nature. In addition, Dostoevsky dramatizes the confession scene so that the reader may understand it both in spiritual and sexual terms. As Raskolnikov prepares to confess to Sonia, he turns pale, sits down on Sonia's bed, and his whole body shivers; at the same time, Sonia begins to pant and her face becomes paler and paler. When Sonia understands that Raskolnikov is the murderer, she shudders convulsively and sinks "helpless on the bed."

The deep grudge that Raskolnikov feels against his mother and in a less intense way against his sister is a grudge against their "love for him and his for them." But the love is not just the sacrificial love of his adult years. Below the sacrificial love there is the original love which he had to bear and struggle against without the aid of the interdicting father. The deep grudge would be then against the repugnant and hateful thing that he had fantasized, and which he had to suffer alone. It is this love which he must punish and for which he must punish himself. It is the hateful mother within him that he attempts to destroy, but which he cannot destroy without destroying himself.

The imagery of the novel and especially of the mare-beating dream suggests a Raskolnikov who attempts frantically and futilely to cut out something repugnant within himself. It is not the pawnbroker or the mother he attempts to kill but the meaning of the hateful mother within him. If he can kill part of himself, he will become whole again; if the hateful and repugnant Raskolnikov can be cut out, the beautiful Raskolnikov will remain. But the hateful thing will not be cut out. The dream of the mare-beating shows us that the punishment creates only more punishment. The dream is not only a symbolic matrix of the contradictory relationships which love occupies in Raskolnikov's conception of himself and his loved ones, but it is also a suggestion of "the cure." It tells us not only what is wrong, but also what will make it right. Raskolnikov not only kills the mare (himself, the pawnbroker, the mother, the landlady), but he also weeps for it and then caresses it and them. The little boy in the dream still exists in the mature Raskolnikov, and it is the little boy that could provide the redemptive strength. What the dream shows symbolically is Raskolnikov—the little boy—kissing (forgiving) the hurt that he is inflicting on the mother-pawnbroker-landlady-sister, and the hurt that Raskolnikov, the adult, inflicts on himself. And this is what the novel shows us, by way of Sonia's intercession: that it will not be by rejection and force that he will be made whole again, but by acceptance-forgiveness: the forgiveness of his mother and of himself, the first step of which is the confession to Sonia. He must come to love and forgive the hateful and repugnant mother within him, and consequently that part of himself; and he does this by way of Sonia, who is not only the religious redemptrice, but also the psychological redemptrice. The hateful mother within him is not only the mother of sacrificial love, but also the mother of sensual love. By loving Sonia, the prostitute, he accepts the dirtiness of love, because it is not actually dirt, no more than it was with his mother, though the phantasies of childhood made it so. Sonia is the living embodiment of "clean" dirtiness, of corruption that is redemptive. She takes him back to his real self and his whole self, not the beautiful and abstract self he had imagined and which he had elevated into grounds for striking out against others and against himself. In order for the mind-soul-psyche to become whole again, the good mother and the hateful mother have to become one, and the good Raskolnikov and the evil Raskolnikov have to become one. What is half-confessed in his dream is wholly confessed to Sonia, and Sonia asks him to do the final thing: to confess it to everyone. What is hidden must become open, because it is by becoming open that the self reclaims itself.

The overt motives Raskolnikov gives to explain the murder of the pawnbroker are rationalizations and, in psychoanalytic terminology, defenses against what he fears is ugly and hateful in himself. Raskolnikov sees himself and wants to be someone free of the old Raskolnikov. The motivations are aspirations in fantasy, yet real as aspiration, to a total freedom. The explanation of the old Raskolnikov, the hateful and repugnant Raskolnikov that I have given in erotic and sexual terms, can be reconverted, if one wishes, into ethical terminology. What he discovers is that he cannot deny the old Raskolnikov, and thus the freedom he aspires to is bought at the price of self-destruction and that "true" freedom is bought at the price of acceptance of the old slavery. Beauty and ugliness, freedom and responsibility become one in the acceptance of oneself. Perhaps this is what Dostoevsky meant by forgiveness and suffering. Such a conversion into ethical terminology—though correct—empties the drama of some of its specific content, for one must still have freedom from what and the acceptance of what slavery? There is enough in the novel to suggest that the specific content, in some part, is erotic and sexual and that the consequent translations of such impulses into guilt and shame come to color the conscious and conventional love of son and mother, brother and sister. The fantasies and experiences of childhood leave deep and ineradicable channels in us, through which flow the experiences we later characterize as religious, social, economic, and practical. It is astonishing that Dostoevsky was able to perceive this dramatically, but it was not astonishing to Freud who, on the occasion of his seventieth birthday paid the extraordinary tribute to Dostoevsky acknowledging, with generosity characteristic of him, that everything he had discovered was already to be found in Dostoevsky's works.

SUMMARY

W. D. Snodgrass in "Crime for Punishment: The Tenor of Part One" made an important contribution to the understanding of Raskolnikov's motives by suggesting that the pawnbroker was a displaced representative of the mother and that Raskolnikov, in killing the pawnbroker, was striking symbolically against the mother. Snodgrass failed to pursue the psychoanalytic implications of this perception and brought back his interpretation of Raskolnikov's motives to familiar moral and psychological conclusions.

The repressed eroticism and hostility that Raskolnikov feels for his mother is expressed more fully and in finer structural detail than Snodgrass suspected: the situations, imagery, and character traits are constructed to move from concealment to overtness as one proceeds from mother to landlady and pawnbroker. Sonia may be considered to be a sexual as well as an ambiguous redemptrice, since she embodies, in Raskolnikov's eyes, "clean-dirtiness." She permits him to come to terms with the hateful and repugnant mother he had fantasized within himself and had attempted unsuccessfully to cut out of himself.

Puzzle and Mystery, the Narrative Poles of Knowing: *Crime and Punishment*

Michael Holquist

The best way to see the biographical dilemma in *Crime and Punishment* is to focus on the distinctive plot of that novel. At first glance it would seem to be the least complex of all Dostoevskian narratives (which is no doubt why *Crime and Punishment* is so frequently called Dostoevsky's "best-made" novel). It is divided into six parts (or books) and an epilogue. In the first part Raskolnikov murders two women; then, in the next five parts, everyone (including Raskolnikov) tries to figure out the crime; in the sixth part Raskolnikov confesses, is tried, and sent to Siberia. In the epilogue he repents of the crime (but only in the second part of the epilogue) and has a mystical experience; the novel ends with the narrator's assertion that "here begins a new story." The murder in the first book, and its consequences in the next five books, constitute *one* kind of time, a pattern made up of one kind of privileged moment and the sequence that flows from it. The conversion in the epilogue and the "new story" it results in constitute *another* kind of temporality, another moment-sequence design.

Dostoevsky stresses that Raskolnikov discovers "another reality" in the concluding pages of *Crime and Punishment*. The argument of this [essay] is that the difference between this reality and that other which dominates in the rest of the novel can best be grasped as the difference between two patterns of moment-sequence: that are dramatized as two different and opposing types of plot and the two different kinds of time, two different ways of understanding, two different modes of interpretation that their

From *Dostoevsky and the Novel*. © 1977 by Princeton University Press.

traditions presuppose. The uniqueness of *Crime and Punishment* consists in the dialectical (or in Bakhtin's sense of the word, the dialogic) structure Dostoevsky has created out of these oppositions.

It has often enough been pointed out that the essential trait of Dostoevskian characters is their duality, the synthesis of extremes present in all of them, which results in dialogic or polyphonic relationships of enormous complexity. As John Bayley has recently said, "[Dostoevsky's] characters . . . [are] all involved in a dream, in a dramatic relation with their own self-awareness . . . [they are both] the insulted and the proud, the hated and the hater. In Dostoevsky the contract is dissolved: its partners become one flesh." There is a sense in which all his characters are "doubles." But behind the psychological unity he creates out of his metaphysically split *characters* is the structural unity of his *plots,* which are also made up of elements that, in the hands of a more conventional novelist, would be clashing, disparate, even mutually exclusive.

As Leonid Grossman long ago pointed out: "The book of Job, the Revelation of St. John, gospel texts, the Epistle of Peter in the New Testament . . . are . . . combined in a manner peculiar to [Dostoevsky], with the newspaper, the anecdote, the parody, the street scene, the grotesque or even the lampoon. He daringly throws into his melting pot more and more new elements . . . the sensations of cheap thrillers and the pages of God-inspired holy books." In another article, one devoted exclusively to Dostoevsky's frequent use of material from the Gothic (Radcliffe, Maturin) and adventure novel (Soulié, Sue), Grossman further documents his author's traffic with such questionable genres: "How did it happen that the lowest genre of [artistic prose] turned out to be the most convenient expression for the creative ideas of an artistic philosopher who was a genius?" In Dostoevsky's novels you get material "ranging from philosophical doctrines to puppet show effects out of the folk theater . . . philosophical dialogue expanded into an epic of adventure; it is the *Phaedo* put at the center of the *Mysteries of Paris,* a mixture of Plato and Eugene Sue." We can, in the case of *Crime and Punishment,* be more specific about the terms of the plot contrasts Dostoevsky uses: what Grossman identifies as the Eugene Sue tendency is present in the six books that constitute the body of the novel as a detective story; the Platonic element is present as a wisdom tale in the epilogue.

I

E. M. Forster once said [in *Aspects of the Novel*] that "in a novel there is always a clock," by which he meant, of course, that just as clocks organize time outside of texts, so does plot within them. Forster later goes on to discuss various kinds of plot, among them one most easily apparent in the detective story: "It occurs through a suspension of the time-sequence; a mystery is a pocket in time . . . half-explained gestures and words, the true meaning of which only dawns pages ahead." The first six books of *Crime and Punishment* constitute a very complicated variant of this narrative type. In order to get at its complexity, some basic considerations about detective plots should be kept in mind.

We may, first, extend Forster's metaphor by recognizing that the distinctiveness of such structures consists in their having not one but *two* clocks. There is [according to Tzvetan Todorov in "The Two Principles of Narrative"] a clock for the crime and another for the solution; one time for the criminal, another for the detective; and the action of the tale consists in the synchronization of the two clocks:

> We know that the [detective novel] is grounded in the tension between two stories: the missing story of the crime, and the presented story of the investigation, the sole justification of which is to make us discover the first story. One element of the story is in fact told to us at the outset: a crime is committed almost under our nose; but we have not learned the identity of the criminals nor the true motives. The investigation consists in reviewing incessantly the same events, in verifying and correcting the tiniest details until, in the end, the truth about this same initial story is revealed.

When the detective's plot (in the sense of beginning, middle, and end) corresponds precisely with the criminal's plot (in the sense of conspiracy), the murder is solved. Another way to articulate this process is to appeal to a distinction often used by the Russian Formalists. All plots can be broken down, or just as significantly, *cannot* be, into *fabula* and *sjužet* (roughly corresponding to Forster's "story" and "plot"). *Fabula* is understood as the chronological sequence of events, 1, 2, 3, 4. *Sjužet* is the way such a chronology is actually arranged in a particular text: 3, 1, 2, 4, for example. Thus it can be said that the distinctive feature of the detective story is that its *sjužet* consists in the discovery of its own *fabula*.

The detective novel then may be said to have two clocks, *but they both tell the same time.* When the detective solves the crime he makes a past event present again, a situation that could be represented as 1, 2, 3, 4, 1′ in which 1 stands for crime, 2, 3, 4, for the detective's attempts to solve it, and 1′ as the crime reconstructed. For the reader, the end (as conclusion) is already present in the beginning; but the end (in the sense of *telos*) is in the *middle* of a detective novel for readers: its whole charm and purpose consist in the process of establishing the correct time (that is why there is usually so much "business" about timetables and diagrams in them). The question is whodunit, but the method is who-was-where-when. The time both of crime and solution, as well as process, in the detective novel, is all cause-and-effect, sequential.

Parallels between the deductive reasoning of detectives and physical scientists have often been noted: both use historical method in the sense that in order to reach conclusions of the sort each desires, they [according to Toulmin and Goodfield in *The Discovery of Time*] "must treat the past as continuous with the present, and interpret the traces left by earlier events in terms of the same laws and principles as apply in the present. As Toulmin and Goodfield have pointed out, in order to "solve" the origin of species or of other natural phenomena, the procedure was the same: "In each case, men grasped the structure of the past only when they took a genuinely historical view; which meant interpreting the present states of Nature and humanity as temporary products of a continuing process developing through time." In other words, the detective, like the scientist, assumes a homogenous time that is as characteristic for the *object* of his study as it is for the *method* of his study; what you get is a temporal democracy in which the past explains the present, which in its turn will one day in the future have the explanatory power of the past. This is a linear or horizontal conception of time and it stands over against another view of temporality that might, by contrast, be called hierarchical or vertical time.

If detective stories are the most elementary expression of horizontal time—horizontal, that is, in the sense that all events occur on the same level of reality—wisdom tales are the most basic index of a time that may be called vertical insofar as it presupposes a split-level ontology, a hierarchy of realities that are distinguished by the degree of stasis that attaches to each. Wisdom tales are understood here as a subdivision within the "simple forms" catalogued by André Jolles, who identifies nine such forms, including proverbs, legends, riddles, etc., as well as the tale (*das Märchen*). Jolles stresses that the tale in its most basic expression is characterized by a strong ethical thrust: the world of which it tells is different from, better than, our own:

> In the tale we are dealing with a form in which what happens, the course of events, is ordered in such a way that it entirely corresponds to the exigencies of naive or unreflexive morality; that is, events are good and just according to the absolute judg-

ment of our feeling. As such the tale puts such events into the most pointed opposition to what we are accustomed to observe—to what, in fact, happens in the world.

Wisdom tales—Midrash, koans, parables from the Bible, Hassidic stories—set themselves off from tales as such in their emphasis on hermeneutics: the distance between the two worlds is affirmed in a structure of conflicting interpretations about what that distance means: the final, "correct" interpretation is superior to the others insofar as it insists on the degree of the cut-off between the two worlds. It is very close to what Jolles calls *Antimärchen*. Whether it is understood as the Augustinian distinction between the Logos of God as opposed to the mere words of men, or the aboriginal Neoplatonism that distinguishes between the Dream Time and everyday flux, such a view assumes that what is most real does not change. All that does change—all that is historical—is meaningful or real only in the degree to which it can be referred back to the privileging stasis. Thus interpretative tales that spring from such a world view tend to have structural affinities with detective stories in that they, too, are characterized by plots that have their end in their beginning. However, when beginning and end are conceived as a nonhistorical alpha and omega, the interest is no longer in the process, the middle. The solution to a detective story exhausts the meaning of what it sets out to understand because its defining act of interpretation is grounded in a temporality that is unitary; criminal and detective act in the same historical reality, and thus logic is the tool of both. That is why so much ingenuity is expended in such tales to establish the equivalence of both, the endless search for an adequate antagonist, a "Napoleon of crime" to test the titan of deduction.

But the wisdom tale, while it frequently has the problem-false-answer-followed-by-correct-solution pattern of detective stories, does *not* treat "the past as continuous with the present and interpret the traces left by earlier events in terms of the same laws and principles as apply in the present." It seeks not to demonstrate a gradual progress unfolding in horizontal time, but to remind men again of the cut-off between vertical levels of temporality, man's change and the Gods' stasis.

Consider an example from Midrash, the body of stories that evolved around attempts to interpret difficult passages in the Torah. Genesis 8:11 says, "And the dove came to [Noah] at eventide; and lo, in her mouth [was] an olive leaf freshly plucked." A gloss on this runs "Whence did she bring it? Rabbi Bebai said: the gates of the garden of Eden opened; she brought it from there. Rabbi Aibo said to him: if she brought it from there, ought she not to have brought something superior, like cinnamon or balsam? But with the olive [the dove] gave a hint to Noah, and said to him: Master Noah, rather this bitter thing from the hand of the Holy One, blessed be he, than a sweet thing from your hand." The structure of this tale—making it typical of such stories—is: there is a problem to be solved; two wise men tell stories that seek to resolve the dilemma. First an answer is given (the olive branch came from Eden). This leads to an incorrect deduction: the dove should have brought cinnamon or balsam. Then the correct answer is given: better a bitter thing, etc. The first answer is logical, assumes that transcendent laws are coterminous with earthly laws, can therefore be solved by reason. But the "correct" answer points to the disparity between the two. The answer to such a puzzle is not a *solution;* rather, it is a reminder of another, and greater, mystery.

The best-known example of this pattern is provided by the contrast between two mysteries in the Oedipus story, the question put by the sphinx and the question of who murdered Laius. Lest the accusation be brought that speaking of Oedipus in connection with tales is to confuse forms, I remind the reader that Jolles himself points to the happy ending of *King Lear* as an example of the "simple form" of the tale once again reasserting its power over the human imagination. Jolles again and again points to the tragic aspects of the split between the ordered world of the tale and the disorder of the world in which it is told: "The tale opposes itself to a world of reality . . . what is tragic, here we may say, is the contention between a world that is naively felt to be moral and the naive ethical demands we make upon what happens." It has been said that Oedipus is the first detective, and in Sophocles' *Oedipus the King* the tragedy opens with the chorus praising the hero for his ability to solve puzzles: you solved the riddle of the sphinx, and moreover, "You did this with no extra knowledge you got from us, you had no training for the task. . . . You are a man of experience, the kind whose plans result in effective action." Oedipus, like so many private detectives, is an amateur (he had no training for the task) who gets results when the professionals (the police), like the seer Tiresias, fail. He sets out to solve the murder in a no-nonsense way, admonishing the chorus "You are praying. As for your prayers, if you are willing to hear and accept what I say now you will find rescue and relief from distress." He attacks the solution Tiresias offers because it is not logical; it is mere priestly mumbo-jumbo: "When the sphinx chanted her riddle here, did you come forward to speak the word that would liberate the people of this town? . . . But you did not come forward, you offered no answer told you by the birds or the Gods. No I came, know-nothing Oedipus, I stopped the sphinx. I answered her riddle with my own intelligence—the birds had nothing to teach me." The seers and their birds, the professionals and their methods, failed to solve the case of the sphinx, and Oedipus in this passage sounds very much like a detective, the genius amateur, boasting of the superiority of his solution (Poirot's little grey cells, Sherlock's repeated, "You know my methods, Watson!"). But the Laius case is more difficult, less amenable to logic. Jocasta says that he conducts the investigation as if he were no longer "a man in control of his reason, judging the present by the past."

But it is just this historical, this deductive, method that assumes horizontal time that Oedipus is, at this point, pursuing: he is attempting to synchronize clocks, to bring past and present into a meaningful congruence. But this time the riddle—in marked contrast to the first problem Oedipus confronts—does not give itself to his reason. It is not Oedipus who solves the crime, but Apollo, as had to be the case because even when all the puzzles in horizontal time had been unravelled, when the story of Oedipus and his true parents and the story of the fight at the crossroads have been reconstructed by deductive means into a true history, the biggest question of all remains: why did these events occur in this way at all? The shape of the events—the chronological reconstruction of who-was-where-when that always is the solution in detective stories—does not in this case constitute an explanation. The historical resolution of the puzzle—it was Oedipus whodunit—simply points to the greater mystery of why it all happened. And in order to answer that question, vertical, extra-human time needs to be broached. The Oedipus story, then, is similar to other wisdom tales in that it is not only about the mystery of fate but an insistence on the Completely Other. Oedipus is taught finally to accept the incommensurability of mere ratiocination, logical deduction (and the historical sense of time that enables it), on the one hand, and, ultimate questions—mysteries not puzzles—on the other.

Lest the emphasis on two opposing grounds of interpretation in Oedipus seem strained it should be remembered that:

The Greek word *Hermeneious* referred to the priest at the Delphic oracle. This word and the more common verb *hermeneien* [to interpret] and noun *hermeneia* [interpretation] point back to the wing-footed messenger-God Hermes, from whose name the words are apparently derived (or vice-versa). Significantly, Hermes is associated with the function of transmitting what is beyond human understanding into a form that human intelligence can grasp. The various forms of the word suggest the process of bringing a thing or situation from unintelligibility to understanding.

(R. E. Palmer, Hermeneutics)

Hermes, as the one who bridges the gap between the language of men and the language of Gods, is a translator. It is not surprising then that wisdom tales that seek to accomplish the hermeneutic task are so full of indirect, metaphorical expression (metaphor from *metaphoreien,* Greek verb "to translate"), even when the translation attempt is to find the one correct meaning for a word out of several that might be possible. Such is the case in Oedipus, where all agree that the ultimate source of meaning is in the Gods; it is Apollo who sends the signs. But the signs themselves are ambiguous, could mean many things. How is one to determine the *single* meaning the Gods intended?

It would seem that insofar as this is the major question in tales presupposing a vertical ontology, another analogue between seer and detective would have made itself apparent. Consider, for example, a Sherlock Holmes story frequently adduced as an example in the modern (as opposed to Tiresias's) study of signs called semiotics, "The Speckled Band." "The Speckled Band" is the last phrase uttered by a woman who dies under mysterious circumstances. No one can figure out what the expression means precisely. Does it refer to the polka-dotted headkerchiefs of the gypsies who are camped near the scene of her death? Or is this the name of a sinister gang? Or a motley musical ensemble? Speckled band is a symbol that could have many meanings, but because Sherlock is able to reduce the ambiguities to the one correct meaning (a snake) he is able to solve the crime.

But this analogue between seer and detective is, of course, only apparent: both are primarily engaged in a hermeneutical task, but each operates out of a different theory of signs. The ground of meaning for the seer is in another reality; he translates from one ontology to another, from the language of Gods to the language of men. The ultimate source of significance for the detective is, however, to be found only in the one ontology, the language of men. He does not translate from another language, he *uncovers (de-tegere)* a meaning that is potentially present in a language *already known.* Thus the means of interpretation will be quite different for each.

The relevance of this distinction for *Crime and Punishment* will perhaps be clearer if we characterize it further along the lines suggested by Paul Ricoeur:

The hermeneutic field is internally at variance with itself . . .

according to one pole, hermeneutics is understood as a manifestation and restoration of a meaning addressed to one in the
manner of a message, a proclamation, or, as is sometimes said,
a *kerygma;* according to the other pole it is understood as a de-
mystification, as a reduction of illusion . . . on the one hand,
purify discourse of its excesses, liquidate the idols, go from
drunkenness to sobriety, realize our state of poverty once and
for all; on the other hand, use the most nihilistic, destructive,
iconoclastic movement so as to *let speak* what once, what each
time was *said,* when meaning appeared anew, when meaning
was at its fullest. Hermeneutics [is] . . . animated by this double motivation: willingness to suspect, willingness to listen,
vow of rigor, vow of obedience.

If wisdom tales and detective stories have in common that they are
both about interpretation, they differ in the fundamental way here characterized by Ricoeur: the wisdom tale, in that it usually seeks to explain a
prior text, Holy Writ, or the saying of an Oracle, attempts to "let speak
what once . . was said . . . when meaning was at its fullest"; its vow of
obedience insures that its explanation will end by insisting on the mysteri-
ousness (for human reason) of the mystery that occasioned it. The tale of
Job would be best illustration. The detective story, on the other hand, is
best "understood as a de-mystification, as a reduction," its explanatory
aim is to show that mystery is an illusion. Any of the Father Brown stories
would serve as clearest example of this tendency.

Now each of these hermeneutic narratives presupposes a different
temporality. The wisdom tale attempts to wipe out time in that the mystery at the end of the plot refers back to the mystery with which it began:
it is a language act performed in time that seeks to dramatize the timeless-
ness of its subject; it is words about the One Word, the Logos. Its end,
both as plot constituent and as telos, is an insistence on the primacy of the
Beginning. It is a sequence about a moment that is privileged vis-à-vis its
own time markers. Just the opposite is the case with detective stories, each
of which is less a "black-mask mystery" than a black-box puzzle, a narrative self-destruct mechanism: the end of its plot is to wipe out its beginning. While, as mentioned earlier, the process, the middle of the story, is
what interests the reader, from the point of view of the plot itself, it is the
end that counts. The end moment is privileged, but only vis-à-vis the *particular* sequence that is the story's plot, not against sequence *as such*. Some
of Sherlock's solutions may be more logically ingenious than others, but
they all depend on sequence, indeed insist on it.

I dwell on these particular aspects of what must seem an obvious contrast because the two attitudes toward interpretation, the two temporalities they presuppose, and the two narrative structures we have been discussing are the determining features, constitute the terms of, the moment-sequence *dominanta* in *Crime and Punishment*. That is to say, if I may recapitulate, that the plot of *Crime and Punishment* is arranged around two moments, each of which is privileged in a different way, and each of which results in a different sequence. The first is the moment of Raskolnikov's crime that occurs in book 1, and the sequence of punishment that flows from it in the following five books. The second is the moment of Raskolnikov's conversion in the epilogue, and the sequence of the "new story" with which the novel ends. The first has the formal properties of a detective story, the second of a wisdom tale.

II

The two clocks of a detective story are represented by two characters, the criminal and the detective. Now to the list of oppositions that is usually invoked to capture the duality of a typical Dostoevskian character (sinner-saint, proud-humiliated, etc.), we must in the case of Raskolnikov add another: he is both hunter and hunted. As happens in such twentieth-century metaphysical detective stories as Robbe-Grillet's *The Erasers,* Borges's "Death and the Compass," or Witold Gombrowicz's "Premeditated Crime," there is a mysterious collusion between detective and murderer; but in each of these examples what is essentially a subject-object dilemma is still neatly divided between two characters. In *Crime and Punishment* the split is internalized in the consciousness of a single protagonist, Rodion Raskolnikov.

He is the criminal, so much is obvious. But he is also victim: on the way to commit the murder he compares himself to a man on his way to execution (part 1, chap. 5); and as he confesses to Sonya later (part 5, chap. 4), "I killed myself, not the old woman." What he means by this is that the man who murdered the pawnbroker *in that act* got rid of the self Raskolnikov conceived himself to be before the act of murder. Raskolnikov's identity is felt by him not to be continuous with itself before and after the crime: after discovering that the role of murderer made his old self a victim, in the first book, Raskolnikov is forced to take up a new role, that of detective of his old self's motive, in order to create a new identity, a new life for himself. If he can understand *why* his old self committed the crime he will know the self whodunit; and insofar as he understands whodunit, he will know who he is.

The crime itself is performed in a fog of uncertainty; everything happens by chance. Raskolnikov acts as if in a delirium; he is constantly surprised to find himself in this or that place, holding the axe, running away. His dreamlike state is dramatized by the narrator's subtle but insistent emphasis on the cut-off between Raskolnikov's hallucinatory uncertainties and the precise chronology of all his movements, which are charted from moment to moment: "Suddenly he heard a clock strike. . . . It seemed to him strange and monstrous that he could have slept in such forgetfulness from the previous day and had done nothing, had prepared nothing yet. . . . And meanwhile . . . it had struck six" (part 1, chap. 6). As he dazedly makes his preparations he hears someone in the yard say, "It struck six long ago," and he says, "Long ago, My God," and rushes out. As he walks to the pawnbroker's apartment, "he saw that it was ten minutes past seven." And then, as he gets there: "here was the house, here was the gate. Suddenly a clock somewhere struck once! What! Can it be half-past seven? Impossible, it must be fast!" After he murders the second woman, Lizaveta, "a sort of blankness, even dreaminess, had begun by degree to take possession of him; at moments he forgot himself." As Raskolnikov later says (part 3, chap. 3): "I remember everything down to the smallest detail, and yet if you were to ask me why I did something, or went somewhere, or said something, I don't think I could give a clear explanation."

The confusion of the crime itself is contrasted in the rest of the novel with Raskolnikov's acute attempts to analyze it. He isolates three different motives, each of which becomes the iconic attribute of a self who is presented as a suspect, only to be cleared in favor of one of the other motive-defined selves. In chapter 4 of part 5 he reviews them all for Sonya. The first is robbery: "It was to rob her." He wanted the money for food, to save his mother from poverty, his sister from being sold to Luzhin. But he quickly dismisses this; he admits he buried the purse he stole without even looking into it: "if I'd killed simply because I was hungry . . . then I should be happy now."

The second motive is one that is much more deeply explored in the novel: "I wanted to make myself a Napoleon, and that is why I killed her." Earlier (part 3, chap. 5) we learn that Raskolnikov's old, pre-murder self had written an article; in it Raskolnikov "developed the idea that all the . . . law-givers and regulators of human society, beginning with the most ancient, and going on to Lycurgus, Solon, Mahomet, Napoleon and so on, were without exception transgressors, by the very fact that in making a new law they *ipso facto* broke an old one, handed down from their fathers and held sacred by society." While such ideas have obvious parallels in Nietzsche's essay "The Uses and Abuses of History," Philip Rahv was surely right to point to the greater fruitfulness of a comparison with Hegel's conception of the world-historical individual: "Dostoevsky gives us a parody-version of Hegel's theory of two types of men [the superior hero and the inferior mass he is to lead] by abstracting [the theory] from its historical logic." Raskolnikov's conception of the murder as a world-historical act is absurd, as he becomes painfully aware. He does so under the shadow of yet another brutalized aspect of Hegel's philosophy of history, an aspect often expressed in Schiller's line, *Weltgeschichte ist Weltgericht,* "world history is the world court." That is, Raskolnikov not only advances as his most programmatically complete reason for *committing* the murder a motive derived from Hegel; he also *judges* his act by appealing to a debased Hegelian principle of interpretation: what succeeds is correct, what fails is wrong. As he says to his sister Dunia (part 6, chap. 7):

> "I shed blood, which flows and has always flowed on this earth
> in torrents, which is poured out like champagne, and for which
> men are crowned in the Capitol and afterwards called benefac-
> tors of mankind. . . . I myself wanted to benefit men, and I
> would have done hundreds, thousands, of good deeds, to make
> up for that one piece of stupidity—not even stupidity, but sim-
> ple clumsiness, since the whole idea was not nearly as stupid as
> it seems now when it has failed (failure makes anything seem
> stupid) . . . if I had succeeded I should have been crowned, but
> now I shall fall into the trap."

Let us recapitulate for a moment: it may be, as G. K. Chesterton had one of his characters say (in "The Blue Cross"), that, "The criminal is the creative artist; the detective only a critic." But even, as in Raskolnikov's case, when—or especially when—artist and critic are one man, a general ground for any specific interpretation is necessary. Raskolnikov committed the murder as in a trance, it is like a dream he must interpret. It is precisely for him the problem as Freud posed it: "The dream as a nocturnal spectacle is unknown to us; it is accessible only through the account of waking hours. The analyst interprets this account, substituting for it another text which is, in his eyes, the thought-content of desire, i.e., what desire would say could it speak without constraint." Raskolnikov, dreamer and analyst, turns for the ground of his interpretation to history: the causes can be known only in their effects. There is nothing higher than history; there is no transcendent, so the truth can be known only retrospectively, in events, as a judgment of historical trial by combat. The shape of events will explain them. As Hegel said, "It was for a while the fashion to admire God's wisdom in animals, plants, and individual lives. If it is conceded that Providence manifests itself in such objects and materials, why not also in world history? . . . Our intellectual striving aims at recognizing that what eternal wisdom *intended,* it has actually *accomplished.*"

Raskolnikov's historicism is important to any understanding not only of his own motives, the thematics of the novel if you will, but also to its morphology. Since Raskolnikov uses historical method in his search for self, he inevitably acts like a detective, interpreting "the traces left by earlier events in terms of the same laws and principles as apply in the present." Since all that is real is rational, and all that is rational real, in Hegel's oft-misunderstood formulation, reason will suffice unto a solution. It is reason that tells Raskolnikov he has failed in his intention to transcend morality; therefore at the end of the novel he turns himself in—he has finally discovered that he is no more than a criminal. The true self has been found, and like the detective story whose temporality it shares, the novel thus can close.

III

But of course there is still the epilogue. In it, as Raskolnikov finds a new conception of time and selfhood, we discover that his Hegelian motive and its consequences are a false solution. Already in the novel proper Raskolnikov had hinted at a reason for his crime other than robbery or a secularized messianism. The murder was simply an extreme situation he sought to exploit in order to find out who he really *was;* as he says—in one of those terrifying Dostoevskian immediacies—"I longed to kill without casuistry, to kill for my own benefit and for that alone! I would not lie about it even to myself! I did not commit murder in order to use the profits and power gained to make myself a benefactor to humanity. Rubbish! I simply murdered; I murdered for myself, for myself alone . . . it was only to *test myself*" (part 5, chap. 4). But of course—given his historical bias—he can only conclude he failed the test. As late as the second chapter of the epilogue Raskolnikov "could find no particularly terrible guilt in his past except a simple blunder . . . he was ashamed he had perished so blindly and hopelessly, with such mute stupidity, by some decree of blind fate and must humble himself and submit to the 'absurdity' of that decree . . . the first steps of [the benefactors of mankind] were successfully carried out, and therefore *they were right,* while mine failed, which means I had the right to permit myself that step." Accepting history as the ultimate source of meaning, he can find no way to appeal its verdict, there is no extra-temporal supreme court; the sequence the moment of his crime has condemned him to is final: "An objectless and undirected anxiety in the present, and endless sacrifice, by which nothing would be gained in the future, was all the world held for him." Raskolnikov had sought to give himself definitive knowledge of his self in the murder; it was an attempt to create a secular *kairos,* a moment that would insure the validity of all his other moments. Among his other dualities, he thus has taken on the roles of both Christ and Lazarus, seeking to gain a new identity by his *own* actions, to bestow a new life through his own mediation. But instead of raising a new self, his old identity is executed in the murder. At the end of the novel, then, he is in the dilemma Hans Meyerhoff has described in connection with Oedipus:

> He is "in fact," that is, in terms of his own experience, two different persons—though in terms of the objective "facts" of Nature and history he is one and the same. We say that Oedipus didn't know who he was, which is correct in that he failed to experience his life under the aspect of temporal continuity . . . the tragedy of Oedipus may still be seen in the light . . . of the fact that the break between his two "pasts" was so severe and the consequences of this split in his personality were so disastrous that it was impossible to mend the broken pieces of the self.

As Maurice Beebe has said, "Raskolnikov commits a murder not that he may be an 'extraordinary' man, but that he *may see* if he is one," and the novel up to its last three pages chronicles the failure of Raskolnikov's gamble in the lottery of selfhood. In those last three pages, however, he is granted another moment, another sequence, as he becomes a character in the wisdom tale with which the epilogue concludes.

It is Easter, time for rebirth. Raskolnikov has just come out of the hospital, where, in his illness, he has had one of those great Dostoevskian programmatic dreams that recapitulates in symbols the meaning of his novelistic actions. He sits by the bank of "the wide, solitary river. From the high bank a broad landscape was revealed. From the other bank far away, was faintly borne the sound of singing. There in the immensity of the steppe . . . it seemed as though . . . *time had stood still,* and the age of Abraham and his flocks was still the present" (emphasis added). Sonya appears and "how it happened he himself did not know, but suddenly he seemed to be seized and cast at her feet . . . *now at last the moment had come*" (emphasis added). What has happened here, of course, is that Raskolnikov has undergone a conversion experience, and even in its small details it is strikingly similar to the source of this and many another examples of the *topos,* the famous scene in the garden at the end of chapter 8 in Augustine's *Confessions:* tears, distant voices, being thrown onto the ground, and inability to speak, this last trait especially significant in the conversion experience because it dramatizes the condition of infancy (*in-fari, infans,* he who does not speak) that is part and parcel of the rebirth that conversion symbolically makes possible.

But in order to be reborn, the old self must die. We are here touching on the main theme of *Crime and Punishment,* as Dostoevsky himself indicated in his notebooks to the novel: under the heading "The Main Idea" (followed by "Eureka!"), he writes: Raskolnikov sees in Sonya "perspectives for a new life and love . . . he finally comes to himself, victorious. From one point of view life has ended, from another, it is beginning." The radical break in identity is present in almost all accounts of conversion (even when they are "secondary conversion") experiences: Augustine, the rhetor, dies, as the future Bishop of Hippo is born; Thomas Aquinas, after his experience, on the Feast of St. Nicholas in 1273, dies as a scholar: "All that I have written seems like straw to me"; and he never wrote another line. In Raskolnikov's case this mystical suppression of self, the death of his old identity ("Love has raised [him] from the dead"), is just as decisive as was the death of an even earlier self, the one that died in the act of murder. Raskolnikov is a completely different person as the epilogue closes: "And what were all, *all* the torments of the past? Everything, even his crime, even his sentence and his exile seemed to him *now* . . . to be something external and strange, as if it had not happened to him at all."

And just as in the confessional mode of autobiography there is a break in the sequence of the self after the *kairotic* moment, so is there a change in the sequence of the telling. Augustine, again, provides a convenient example: to the moment of conversion, the tale of his life advances more or less chronologically, as an autobiography; but after the crucial moment in the Roman garden is recounted (and its immediate after-effects), the historical progression ceases, we are given no more biographical details for the fourteen years intervening between the mystical experience in Rome and the written account of it in the *Confessions.* Instead, the concluding chapters are devoted to a meditation on time and memory, and it closes with a reading of the book of Genesis. It, too, *ends* with an interpretation of a text that is about ultimate beginnings. After conversion, all else is felt to be anticlimactic, the ensuing series of discreet moments is already fore-shadowed in that one moment. Augustine's first four books cover twenty-eight years, but the next five books treat only *four* years, climaxing in his conversion. The last four books abandon chronology altogether. What is significant is precisely the rupture between old and new identity, the meaning of the self in its discontinuity:

> It is the internal transformation—which furnishes a subject for a narrative discourse in which "I" is both subject and object. . . . It is because past "I" is different from the present "I" that the latter may really be confirmed in all his preroga-tives. The narrator describes not only what happened to him at a different time in his life, but above all how he became—out of what he was—what he presently is . . . the deviation, which establishes the autobiographical reflection, is thus double: it is at once a deviation of time and identity.

This deviation in *Crime and Punishment* is experienced as a felt discon-tinuity between the narrative mode of the novel, on the one hand, and its epilogue, on the other. All readers of the book have sensed this disjunc-tion, many objecting to the forced or tacked-on quality of the ending, usu-ally because they assume Dostoevsky was striving for a conventional nar-rative homogeneity. But if we assume on the contrary that he seeks to accentuate, to dramatize, the differences between the two parts of the book, the shape of the text assumes another kind of unity.

The whole novel is an account of Raskolnikov's various attempts to forge an identity for himself with which he can live. From the very begin-ning of the novel he has sought a means to justify his existence or, in the language of the text, to find a faith. Porfiry Petrovich underscores this thirst for validity: the investigator says: "Do you know how I regard you? As one of those who would allow themselves to be disembowelled, and stand and face their torturers with a smile—if they had found a faith" (part 6, chap. 2). All Raskolnikov's actions—his article on new lawgivers (who found a new faith), the murder itself, and his attempts to understand it—are probes toward a moment that will give lasting meaning to the rest of his life.

He is like the underground man in that he seeks a plot in which to become a character, a shape that will endow each of his discreet actions with an end. But *unlike* the underground man he attempts to ground his identity, not in fictive plots, but rather in historical narratives. The six parts of the novel tell how Raskolnikov, who feels he is existentially out of place in the historical context of nineteenth-century Russian society, tries to create a *new* historical sequence, as had Solon, Mahomet, etc. Like a tragic Baron Munchhausen, he seeks to pull himself out of the swamp of time by his own metaphysical pigtail. But he discovers that he is not a world historical individual; he is not a character in *that kind* of a history. It is only in the epilogue that he discovers the kind of narrative that is properly his own to live: it is not a secular history to which he belongs, but a wisdom tale.

Dostoevsky treats Raskolnikov as Stephen Marcus has suggested Freud dealt with his patients:

> Freud is implying that a coherent story is in some manner connected with mental health . . . and this in turn implies assumptions of the broadest and deepest kind about the nature of coherence and the form and structure of human life. . . . At the end—at the successful end—one has come into possession of his own story. It is a final act of self-appropriation, the appropriation by oneself of one's own history.

As narrator, Dostoevsky assigns values to the various characters according to the decree they are successful in merging their character with a plot that is adequate to it. Thus Lebezyatnikov is a gentle, naive person, a utopian socialist nevertheless who seeks to live out a scenario of tough-minded nihilism that results in such absurdities as his assumption that Sonya has become a prostitute as a protest against society. Marmeladov's drunkenness, his wife's insanity, are the consequences of biographical failures of emplotment: he cannot live the role of philosopher; she cannot live that of a grand dame. Svidrigailov is a gambler, possibly a double murderer (of his manservant and his wife), and a sensualist who violates young girls. Yet the story into which he wishes to insert himself, a parody of the golden-hearted prostitute cliché, is one in which, by forcing Dunia to marry him (at gun point), he will be saved, can settle down to a quiet life of domestic bliss. The consequences of failing to arrive at a workable assimilation of character and plot are severe—Svidrigailov cannot make his *happy* ending work, so is (self) condemned to death—the "correct" ending for the character he has played all his life. He has lived the role of villain in a realistic novel, and because he cannot become the hero of a sentimental story, he dies.

Over against these failures stand those figures who have come to know themselves—or, in the terms we have been using, come to know the story to which their character corresponds. Porfiry Petrovich is able to sum up his whole life with conviction and modesty: "Who am I? I am a man who has developed as far as he is capable, that is all!" He goes on to make the distinction between himself and Raskolnikov: "But you—that's another matter" and suggests that Raskolnikov will "pass into a different category of men" (part 5, chap. 2). It is the same distinction Raskolnikov will make in connection with Sonya: "You too have stepped over the barrier . . . you were able to do it. You laid hands on yourself, you destroyed a life . . . *your own*" (part 4, chap. 4). He recognizes that she has risen again, lives as a character in the Lazarus story she reads to him—even before he has been able to enter that same story himself, because he still sees himself in the light of historical narrative at this point in the novel. But after his conversion, the Lazarus plot will be his as well.

The deviation between "normal" lives and the one led by Raskolnikov is marked not only in a thematic distinction between his own old self and the new one he discovers, but in the difference between the formal properties of the detective story plot he lives in the novel and the formal properties of the wisdom tale, in which be becomes a character in the novel's epilogue. Thematically *Crime and Punishment* is the account of Raskolnikov's search for a story that will endow his life with validity. He first seeks such a narrative structure in a theory of history that is recognizably Hegelian and unquestionably secular. He kills in order to test whether he is, or is not, an instrument of historical change: since there is nothing higher than history itself, you can know its judgments only after having acted. Having committed the murder, he discovers he is in fact not a character in the drama of historicism. In order, then, to establish a continuity in his identities, to reassemble the shattered "I" destroyed in the outcome of the crime, he seeks the existential glue of another kind of story. But since historicism is the source of the murder—and of the confusion following upon it until Raskolnikov turns himself in—this part of the narrative is told in a way that employs many of the features of a detective story, since, as R. G. Collingwood has pointed out:

> There is nothing other than historical thought itself, by appeal to which its conclusions may be verified. The hero of a detective novel is thinking exactly like an historian when, from indications of the most varied kinds, he constructs an imaginary picture of how a crime was committed, and by whom. At first this is a mere theory awaiting verification, which must come to

it from without. Happily for the detective, the conventions of
that literary form dictate that when his construction is complete, it shall be neatly pegged down by a confession from the
criminal, given in such circumstances that its genuineness is beyond question.

(*The Idea of History*)

Since an authentic self is the object of Raskolnikov's various attempts
to explain why he committed the murder (if he understands *why*-dunit,
he'll know *who*-dunit), it is clear that his first public confession—which
ends the novel proper—is an unsatisfactory solution. A self-construction
has *not* been "neatly pegged down by a confession from the criminal."
Raskolnikov exhausts the detective story formula without achieving its
benefit—a complete resolution of the mystery that sets the story going. If
we invoke the metaphor with which we began, the two clocks of the plot
fail to synchronize. Thus, after his trial, it is said of Raskolnikov (now in
Siberia): "An objectless and undirected anxiety in the present, and endless
sacrifice, by which nothing would be gained, in the future—that was all
the world held for him" (epilogue, chap. 2).

Raskolnikov has failed to find a self in the detective story into which
his attempt to enter historical narrative has devolved; but another plot is
vouchsafed to him, as we saw, in the epilogue's last pages—another time
is broached. The last pages of the novel are not only *about* another time;
they are told in a different time: the movement from the dream to the final
word of the text is constituted in a manner that sets it off from the body
of the novel insofar as it tells of years in sentences, while in the body of the
text minutes are told in pages. This has disturbed such readers as Ernest J.
Simmons: "Following the line of least resistance, [Dostoevsky] often ignored the time-sequence. In one of the notebooks he boldly declares
'What is time? Time does not exist; time is a cipher; time is the relation
of being to unbeing.' " Exactly—and that is why, far from "following the
line of least resistance," Dostoevsky is at great pains to emphasize the difference between the time of the novel, whose hundreds of pages tell of
only two weeks (the crucial part 1 tells of only three days), while the last
paragraph of the epilogue covers the rest of Raskolnikov's life. Since
Raskolnikov has found his self, he has entered what Dostoevsky always
called "living life" (*Živaja' žizn'*): the relation between mere flux—unbeing—and the nonchanging significance of the being he discovers in the
moment of his conversion results in a diminished significance for chronol-

ogy. This is not the historical or even psychological time of the Bergsonian *durée* variety—it is time understood precisely as "the relation of being to unbeing."

IV

If, as we have suggested, there is a disjunction between the temporal structure of the novel proper and its epilogue, does this mean—as many readers have felt—that there is a break in the unity of *Crime and Punishment*? The suggestion of this [essay] has been, rather, that there is a bond between the parts, a bond that derives from the direction of time in the two story types that define the novel, on the one hand, and the epilogue, on the other. The detective story properties shaping Raskolnikov's search for identity in the novel tend toward a conclusion that will resolve all the mysteries.

But it does not, because in the course of his investigation Raskolnikov has, in his obsessive honesty, raised the question of evil, and, as H. R. Niebuhr has said [in *The Nature of Religious Experience*], "the mystery of good and evil in human life and in the world cannot be completely comprehended as stated in perfectly logical terms." What the theologian here states is the ancient message of the wisdom tale: "Knowest thou the ordinance of heaven? Canst thou set the dominion thereof in the earth?" The movement of the epilogue is analogous to the wisdom tale in that it points back to the inadequacy of answers that precede its concluding insistence on *another* realm, *another* time: the "correct" answer is not a solution, but the reminder of another and greater mystery. Thus the historical movement of the novel is a necessary step toward the debunking of its assumptions in the epilogue. The Underground Man, who never found a plot, is therefore condemned to a dreary life of "bad infinity," and endless succession of empty moments. Thus the formal conclusion of the Dostoevskian plot that contains him is a note from the editor who says "the 'notes' of this paradoxalist do not end here." Whereas *Crime and Punishment* may conclude with a "new tale"—Raskolnikov has found a role for himself in the detective-story-become-wisdom-tale that defines the Dostoevskian plot containing him.

*C*rime and Punishment:
Christianity and Existentialism

A. D. Nuttall

What then is excluded by our Christian reading of *Crime and Punishment*? I answer: Razumikhin, Svidrigailov and Raskolnikov's failure to repent.

Of these, Razumikhin, Raskolnikov's student friend, is the least important. The problem can be stated very simply. According to the picture we have so far built up, the prerational freedom of the existentialist is opposed to Christian love and goodness. But Razumikhin is an existentialist, and he is good.

Many of Razumikhin's sentiments exactly mirror those of the Underground Man. For example, he is angered almost to violence by those who oppose individualism and is himself a resolute opponent of mechanistic socialism. His existentialism can assume a curiously pure and rigorous form in which the academic philosophy of Sartre is partly anticipated. Just as Sartre in his two books on the imagination laid great stress on man's ability to think what is *not* the case, and found in this our unique freedom, so Razumikhin argues that it is through error that we are human, and then adds an ethical corollary: "To go wrong in one's own way is better than to go right in someone else's. In the first case you are a man, in the second you're no better than a bird." Had Raskolnikov or the Underground Man been the speaker of these lines, we would have had not "bird" but "insect" in the second sentence. The imagery is brightened, it would seem, by the general buoyancy of Razumikhin's character.

But, bright or dark, the ethically revolutionary force of these words

From *Crime and Punishment: Murder as Philosophic Experiment.* © 1978 by A. D. Nuttall. Sussex University Press, 1978.

is undeniable. W. H. Auden, in an essay, saw this revolution as occurring not just in the minds of stray individuals but in the consciousness of nations. He called it the surrender of *Romanitas,* Rome being for him the embodiment of a civic, essentially public responsibility. The Americans, he said, in believing that it was better to do wrong freely than to do right under compulsion had made this crucial surrender. Certainly, applying this lesson of Raskolnikov's own spiritual progress we might be forgiven for seeing in these words the foundation of utter immoralism; better an "authentic" Hitler than an "inauthentic" bourgeois. But then we remember that Razumikhin is not only opposed to mechanistic socialism; he is also, in a manner, opposed to Raskolnikov. Raskolnikov's claim that the *conscience* of the exceptional man could sanction bloodshed shocks and repels Razumikhin. And this surely provides us with the clue we need. Razumikhin's libertarian pronouncements, whatever the degree of formal radicalism they may attain, hold no sting, so to speak, because Razumikhin himself is so incorrigibly kind. His vision of freedom is really a symptom of innocence. It is only because he can hardly conceive of a vicious or cruel use of freedom that he can commend it without reserve. Dounia, who loves Razumikhin and is herself entirely good, sees this. Her first response to his wild imaginings is a mixture of humane assent and intellectual reservation: "Yes, yes . . . though I don't agree with you in everything."

Yet it does not seem quite right to conclude that Razumikhin's existentialist extravagance is acceptable only because it is meaningless. Dostoevsky never patronises his own characters in quite that way. There remains an element of attraction in Razumikhin's dream of freedom. We must be content to say that in him the doctrine remains untested.

Where then does the true test come? Who in the book both preaches and practises a genuinely unfettered freedom? Razumikhin may echo Raskolnikov's doctrines but he does so lightly, and we are undisturbed. But the man who haunts Raskolnikov, who mirrors both his thoughts and his worst actions, is Svidrigailov.

Svidrigailov is what is called a "Dostoevskian double"; that is, a figure deliberately paralleling that of the main character, confronting him with an answering image of his own mind. It is sometimes suggested that Dostoevsky, in adopting this device, anticipated the Freudian division of the unified psyche into a dialectical opposition of ego and id, conscious and unconscious. This view will scarcely survive an attentive reading of Dostoevsky. The Freudian unconscious is prelogical, appetitive, and lies "deeper in," so to speak, than the conscious. The Dostoevskian double, conversely, tends to carry to their logical conclusion ideas conceived in the mind of the principal character; like an extra limb, in rational, Cartesian obedience, he executes the dictates of the hero's mind with a consistency which shocks the original conceiver. Thus, in *The Brothers Karamazov* Ivan's double, Smerdyakov, acting on Ivan's proposition, "Everything is permitted," murders their common father, Fyodor Karamazov. The Dostoevskian double is not so much "deeper in" as "further out."

We first hear of Svidrigailov in the letter Raskolnikov receives from his mother near the beginning of the novel. She explains how Dounia, Raskolnikov's sister, has had to leave the Svidrigailov household because the master of the house had conceived a violent passion for her. Dounia's predicament had been the more difficult in that the mistress of the house, Marfa Petrovna, believed that Dounia was herself a willing party to the affair. Even in the sketchy narrative of a letter Svidrigailov already possesses a special potency, which consists in great strength allied with the purest caprice. His behaviour to Dounia is at first sneering and facetious, then passionately sensual and at last (when he shows his wife the letter which clears Dounia of all guilt) almost chivalrous. Some hint of the Dionysiac, pagan power we are to see later at closer quarters is present in the imagery of the letter, with its apparently trivial reference to "the influence of Bacchus." We sense that the manner of Svidrigailov's drunkenness is very different from the manner of Marmeladov's drunkenness. His very forename—Arkady—evokes, a world at once golden and pre-Christian. Svidrigailov's past, unlike Raskolnikov's, is not intellectual but military. As the story unfolds he moves closer and closer to us. It is not until the last part that we see his face:

> It was a strange face, like a mask; white and red, with bright red lips, with flaxen beard, and still thick flaxen hair. His eyes were somehow too blue and their expression somehow too heavy and fixed. There was something awfully unpleasant in that handsome face, which looked so wonderfully young for his age.

The description is immensely powerful, though the associations it calls up are fugitive: Santa Claus? Some curly bearded Jupiter painted on a fairground stall? Or (still more remote, but obstinately present to this reader's mind) God the Father from the hand of mad William Blake?

What exactly in the world of facts makes Svidrigailov so transcendently evil is difficult to pin down with certainty. It may well be that this is the source of as much strength as weakness. Dostoevsky in the surviving notebooks for *Crime and Punishment* was at one stage much exercised as to how he was to convey the character of Svidrigailov without his novel becoming "unchaste." In the event Dounia's shudder at the mention of his name conveys exactly what is needed. To be sure there is the affair of the serf Philip. Svidrigailov, asked by Raskolnikov whether he believes in ghosts, tells how shortly after the burial of his serf "Filka," he called for his pipe and the man appeared with a hole in the elbow of his coat. Svidrigailov observes, "we had a violent quarrel just before his death." A little later Pulcheria Alexandrovna, Raskolnikov's mother, tells the story to Dounia as she had it from Marfa Petrovna. The story goes that there was indeed a serf called Philip and that he died of ill-treatment (here the story of the ghost begins to take on the atmosphere of Crabbe's *Peter Grimes*). Although Philip killed himself it was "perhaps" Svidrigailov that drove him to it. A similarly powerful suspicion and a similar withholding of final certainty surround the rape of the deaf and dumb girl of fifteen who was found hanged in the garret. All this is of course a fairly elementary manipulation of the reader's fears. The indefinitely horrible is always more frightening than the definitely horrible, in fiction at least.

But when we come to Raskolnikov's dreadful dream in which the murder is reenacted, a higher artistry governs the function in the story of Svidrigailov. Raskolnikov awakens, "but his dream seemed strangely to persist: his door was flung open and a man whom he had never seen stood in the doorway watching him intently." It is his first meeting face to face with Svidrigailov. A friend of mine once described to me the worst dream he ever had. In the dream he was being pursued by something so horrible that years afterwards in recounting the dream he did not care to describe it. At last, however, his eyes opened and he saw the sunlight from the open window shining on the flowered paper of the bedroom wall. Relief flooded through him. Then the bedroom door opened and the thing that had been chasing him came in. And then he *really* woke up. Dostoevsky's narrative, with its momentary sense of the dream persisting, catches something of the special horror of this experience. My friend believes that he momentarily opened his eyes, registered the appearance of his bedroom, and then fell back into the dream. Raskolnikov's case is in a way the opposite. He really awakes, really sees his room and what is actually standing in the doorway, but finds in what he sees no soothing antidote for nightmare, but instead a further terror.

Indeed Svidrigailov the murderer and rapist is never as frightening as Svidrigailov the watcher and listener. To learn that the whole of Raskolnikov's confession to Sonia was overheard by Svidrigailov is at once disgusting and alarming. For a literary precedent one must turn to *Les Liaisons Dangéreuses,* or even to *Othello.* Our modern term for that which engages the mind in a wholly neutral fashion—"interesting"—is absent from Shakespeare's vocabulary, but if it had been present, Iago would have used it. Svidrigailov's reaction to what he hears pass between Raskolnikov and Sonia is very Iago-like:

> But all that time Mr Svidrigailov had been standing listening at
> the door of the empty room. . . . The conversation had struck
> him as interesting and remarkable.

Svidrigailov lives the life implied by Raskolnikov's most fundamental theory. He oversteps, innovates, moves in any direction. His life is the endless utterance of a new language. One is tempted to say that he is the better existentialist of the two but the word "existentialist" implies the intellectual acceptance of a theory, and Svidrigailov derives much of his power from the fact that he is unfettered by theory. We have already seen in the Underground Man how this particular sort of existentialism is essentially self-destructive. The theory proposes a pure spontaneity, but no one can be purely spontaneous who acts to demonstrate a theory. Raskolnikov in soliloquy desperately acknowledges that he cannot attain transcendent freedom, that he is, after all, no better than a louse: "what shows that I am utterly a louse is that . . . *I felt beforehand* that I should tell myself so *after* killing her. . . . The vulgarity! The abjectness!" Raskolnikov is trapped in his own endlessly rationalising consciousness. All the time, both in prospect and retrospect, he is *constructing* his own life as a story, and the whole point about the freedom he desires is that it must not be constructed in this way. Svidrigailov is free from this itch. He is not constantly saying to himself and to others, "Look how unpredictable I am." He lives without casuistry.

There is a remarkable moment in the novel when the theorising Raskolnikov attempts to talk philosophy with his unfettered shadow. From Raskolnikov there comes, with all the anguish of an incorrigibly moral soul, a philosophic denial of Christian doctrine: "I don't believe in a future life." We wait for Svidrigailov's answer, expecting . . . what? A more radical scepticism still? What we get is infinitely stranger than that, though at the same time entirely appropriate to his nature:

> "And what if there are only spiders there, or something of
> that sort?" he said suddenly. "He is a madman," thought
> Raskolnikov. "We always imagine eternity as something be-

yond our conception, something vast, vast! But why must it be vast? Instead of all that, what if it's one little room, like a bath house in the country, black and grimy and spiders in every corner, and that's all eternity is? I sometimes fancy it like that."

Svidrigailov simply refuses to play the philosophic game, he will not theorise. Instead his reply is almost idiotic, artlessly appalling. In moving from Raskolnikov's words to Svidrigailov's, we leave the universe of reasoned discourse, in which certain concepts are stable, to the mean yet terrible world of a Kafka story. Raskolnikov's answer is interesting: "Can it be you can imagine nothing juster and more comforting than that?" This, from the free-thinker!

But if Svidrigailov is as we have described him, what has happened to our picture of *Crime and Punishment* as showing the essential servitude of existential freedom? If we had only Raskolnikov to deal with, that position would be secure. But with the smiling figure of Svidrigailov watching us from the shadows as we watched Raskolnikov in the novel, a different hypothesis presents itself. Raskolnikov reverted to Christian values, not because the other path is intrinsically impassable, but simply because he, personally, lacked the strength to follow it. Doubtless his final submission shows more virtue, more goodness than his rebellion, but then virtue of that kind was never required of the existential hero. The implication is clear: Raskolnikov is an existential failure, and we know this because, stalking behind him through the novel is the living embodiment of existential success.

But, it will be said, Svidrigailov is driven to suicide. Is this freedom? The answer is: perhaps, yes. But we must tread carefully.

Certainly Svidrigailov's final state is a kind of despair. He says to Raskolnikov, "If only I'd been something, a landowner, a father, a cavalry officer, a photographer, a journalist . . . I am nothing." He has named indifferently some things which he has in fact been and others which, as far as we know, he has not. But the central intuition is at last the purest, Sartrian existentialism. It is also the centre of his despair. He also fears death. It remains to ask whether Svidrigailov's perception of this dreadful truth diminishes or enhances his heroic stature *seen from the existentialist point of view*. If we take a moment to compare the cold candour of his intelligence at this point with the endless confused moralising of Raskolnikov, we must grant that his stature is if anything enhanced. So with the suicide. Svidrigailov admits to a great fear of death, but when Raskolnikov in prison looked back on the suicide he saw this too as increasing rather than lowering the stature of the suicide. It may be said: Dostoevsky was a Christian; read his journalism; there can be no serious doubt but that Svidrigailov's suicide was intended to be read as a confession of spiritual bankruptcy. But questions of this sort are not so easily settled. Dostoevsky's journalism, certainly, is more doctrinally univocal than his novels. It is also less intelligent, less rich. In the circumstances it is folly to allow the journalism any sort of jurisdiction over the novels, to flatten the ambiguities of the great work into the simplicity of the lesser. In the second place we are confronted here with the special difficulties which arise when the situation is not only ambiguous in itself, but is presented to us under two different systems of interpretation. There is indeed no doubt that by Christian standards Svidrigailov fails. The point is so obvious as to be scarcely worth making. It seems at least possible that by the philosophy he represents he succeeds. At least, he does if his action is free.

Surely, if Dostoevsky wished to make the Christian principle the unquestioned victor in the novel, his opportunity lay here. To show Svidrigailov hunted to his death, and subdued, would have been to show the existentialist principle defeated at its strongest point. But he did not write it in that way.

Let us look first at the part played by imagery. In *Crime and Punishment* we can distinguish two levels at which imagery operates. First there is the high cultural level of scriptural images, highly explicit, exemplified most powerfully in the references to Lazarus. These we have already noticed. Then there is a level of imagery which is much less explicit, but equally potent. This second level is largely concerned with our sense of space. Thus Raskolnikov is repeatedly associated with suffocating, tiny spaces, with cramped living quarters and narrow streets. At one point he compares his confined existence with that of a spider. His words recall Svidrigailov's vision of a horribly reduced eternity. It is as if we have glimpsed, not the sublime Inferno of Dante, but Hell as it actually is. The impression made by this spatial imagery is so intense that it is difficult to remember that St Petersburg (the novel's setting), though it has its share of narrow streets and tenements is also a city of immense squares and noble boulevards. Most English-speaking readers of *Crime and Punishment* come away from the book fully believing that St Petersburg is a city like London, as drawn by Doré. But the careful reader will soon perceive that in fact the effect is not ubiquitous, but is on the contrary carefully reserved for Raskolnikov. Sonia, who might have been expected to lodge in a small room, has in fact an oddly shaped but very large room. It seems as if Dostoevsky felt some fundamental need to differentiate her habitual spatial environment as strongly as possible from Raskolnikov's, as some sort of objective correlative to their respective spiritual conditions. Even the old pawnbroker, wretched herself and a cause of wretchedness in others, lives in a bright sunlit room (the brightness, Raskolnikov surmises, is probably the work of her sister Lizaveta). But although the claustrophobic imagery of *Crime and Punishment* is directed straight to Raskolnikov, others feel it when they draw near him. His mother, Pulcheria Alexandrovna, remarks on leaving his flat, "If he gets out and has a breath of air . . . it is fearfully close in his room. . . . But where is one to get a breath of air here? The very streets here feel like shut-up rooms." Both Svidrigailov and Porfiry, the two watchers of Raskolnikov, observe at different times with an apparent inconsequence that what he most needs is fresh air.

The Christian interpretation of the meaning of this imagery would appear at first to be quite straightforward: existential freedom is really not freedom but servitude. Is there not a delicious (and profound) irony in the moment when Raskolnikov thinks of dropping his plan, and experiences *that* as freedom? On his way to commit the murder, does he not compare his state to that of a man led to execution (a point on which Dostoevsky could speak with special authority)? Did he not feel his "mind clouded"? Just before, when he learned that Alyona was to be alone and that his opportunity was perfect did he not feel, in flat opposition to his grand theory, that his freedom had been taken from him? The case seems marvellously complete. But what, then, of Svidrigailov?

If the lesson of the Raskolnikov spatial imagery is that his crime was the quintessence of unfreedom, what by parity of reasoning are we to make of the suicide of Svidrigailov? The Christian interpretation of *Crime and Punishment,* as we have seen, really needs here a similar bias in the narrative technique. But instead we are given water, space and air. If confinement means servitude, these must imply the purest freedom.

The story of Svidrigailov's suicide begins with him looking very unimpressive. Before he picks up the gun, "a strange smile contorted his face, a pitiful, sad, weak smile, a smile of despair." He goes then to a pleasure garden, and for a while the general atmosphere of meanness is kept up. But, as he rises to leave, the hot night is split by the sound of thunder and torrential rain falls. It is difficult to convey the full force in the novel of this simple change in the weather. This, we know, is air which Raskolnikov will never breathe, and we open our lungs to it in gratitude. The rain soon gives way to a roaring wind and there in the middle of the windy night we see Svidrigailov crossing the bridge between Vassilyevsky

Island and the mainland. But Svidrigailov passes out of this great wind into a tiny cramped hotel room. Here we may suppose the alternative imagery of confinement is after all to assert itself; but the image will not hold. It is as if one half of Dostoevsky's mind is struggling to tie down Svidrigailov, but the imagery has developed a life of its own and will not be stilled. The effects which follow are those of nightmare. The hotel room in which he finds himself does not after all enclose him. There is a crack in the wall through which he can see, with preternatural clarity, what is happening in the next room. Svidrigailov lies down to sleep, and the room around him seems to become increasingly frail and insubstantial as he listens with dread to the roaring wind and the trees tossing in the darkness. At last he falls asleep but then awakes abruptly. Now the images of wind and air bifurcate. Svidrigailov in utter horror at all around him imagines a cottage on a summer day with the wind strewing the flowers in the window, but then his imagination escaping his control presents him with the horror of death, the corpse of a girl, lying in the middle of this delicious place. He shakes himself free of this unhappy state between dream and reality, crosses the room to the window and flings it wide open. The wind blows in and stings his face, and he becomes aware that there must be a garden beneath the window. And now the imagery begins once more to cohere; what was vertiginous and nauseating a moment before becomes once more invigorating. He hears in the night the boom of the cannon which says that the river is overflowing its banks—overflowing . . . overstepping. He determines to go out and to *choose* as the scene of his suicide "a great bush there, drenched with rain, so that as soon as one's shoulder touches it, millions of drops drip on one's head." But one last horror still awaits him. As he leaves his room and finds his way along the dark passage he comes upon a little girl, crying and cold. He comforts her and to warm her lays her in his own bed. Then she turns to him a face of unmistakable lasciviousness. And then he—again?—wakes up, once more in the hotel bed. The special horror of the dream which involves itself with the waking surroundings, formerly applied to Raskolnikov, is here given a further twist as it is used to torture Svidrigailov. Did he then never awake and throw the window open? Was that, too, part of the dream? We cannot tell. Now, at all events, he can really go out. It is now morning and a milky mist is in the air. He steps out and walks till he finds himself outside a great house with a tower and massive gates. Leaning against the gatepost is a man, dressed in a soldier's coat and "Achilles" helmet, with a drowsy, peevish Jewish face. He "challenges" Svidrigailov:

"What do you want here?"

"Nothing brother, good morning," answered Svidrigailov.

"This isn't the place."

"I am going to foreign parts, brother."

"To foreign parts?"

"To America."

"America?"

Svidrigailov took out the revolver and cocked it. Achilles raised his eyebrows.

"I say, this is not the place for such joke!"

"Why shouldn't it be the place?"

"Because it isn't."

"Well, brother, I don't mind that. It's a good place. When you are asked, you just say he was going, he said, to America." He put the revolver to his right temple.

"You can't do it here, it's not the place," cried Achilles, rousing himself, his eyes growing bigger and bigger.

Svidrigailov pulled the trigger.

When Raskolnikov killed another, he hardly knew what he was doing; when Svidrigailov kills himself he makes an existential joke. Having ridden out the storm of the night, he is confronted by a sort of parody of his regimental past, a castle which is not really a castle, a sentry who is not exactly a sentry, and a posture of witless intransigence which is a perfectly genuine feature of military life. Dostoevsky himself drops into a style of Victorian facetiousness, calling the man "Achilles" after his helmet. To the reiterated words "This is not the place" Svidrigailov returns enigmatic answers. The man, at this time in the morning anyway, is a simply programmed organism; this is not the place—for what? For whatever Svidrigailov is looking for. For making jokes. For shooting yourself.

The number of jokes is said to be rather small, the number of variations infinite. Svidrigailov says ironically that he is going to America, to the new found land. It is likely enough that part of him is certain, as he speaks, that he is going to the old dark place, the place of the spider, to Hell. The guard says "This is not the way." Svidrigailov's answer is really a variation of the ancient answer *Facilis descensus Averni:* "Easy is the Descent into Hell." These were the words of Sibyl used to Aeneas when he was looking for a way into the dark world of the dead. It is not always remembered that Virgil borrowed the phrase not from Homer but from the comic writer Aristophanes; the phrase, long before Virgil, had begun *as a joke*: "How do I get into Hades?" asks Dionysus in *The Frogs*. "Easy," is the answer, "just jump off that cliff or hang yourself from that tree." "This is not the place," says the guard to Svidrigailov. "Easy," says the crack of the gun as the bullet enters Svidrigailov's skull. They later found in Svidrigailov's notebook a few words in explanation of his suicide; they said that he died *in full possession of his faculties* and no one was to blame for his death.

The contrast with Raskolnikov remains overwhelming. I do not argue that the wind and weather that attend on Svidrigailov's death are uniformly delightful. Manifestly, they carry both relief and terror. I claim only a fundamental antithesis. Heat, confinement and suffocation are one thing; wind, rain and morning mist are another. If the former mean the denial of freedom, the latter must, by the language of images we have learned, mean freedom; freedom with all its horror, but the real thing. We may say of Svidrigailov what was once said of another inhabitant of Hell:

> *E parve di costoro*
> *Quegli che vince e non colui che perde.*

We now have the material for the existentialist interpretation of *Crime and Punishment*. The breaking of Raskolnikov no longer demonstrates the hollowness of existentialism, but only the weakness of Raskolnikov. The story of *Crime and Punishment* now becomes the story not of a man's descent into hell and rebirth into glory, but of a failure. Raskolnikov tried to be free, but was sucked back into the mire of ethics and all the complex apparatus assembled by the Church for the diminution of humanity. Dostoevsky wrote in the first notebook for *Crime and Punishment,* "Sonia and Love broke him."

But what of the language of the epilogue—"resurrection," "regeneration"? At all this the existentialist reader will merely smile: "With such goodies the renegades from truth are commonly rewarded." What then of the despair of Svidrigailov? Again the distant smile: "We never said the truth was easy to bear. Our philosophy was not formed to console but to confront. We note only that in Svidrigailov's case the truth is borne, and in Raskolnikov's it is not. Svidrigailov kills himself but at least he is the author of his action."

We all know that Dostoevsky, were he a party to this debate, would support the Christian interpretation and attack the existentialist. Yet in a curious way it is the existentialist interpretation which best "preserves the phenomena." The Christian reading is constantly embarrassed—by Razumikhin, by Svidrigailov, but the existentialist reading is utterly unembarrassed. Moreover, the imagery of the book works harder for the existentialist than the Christian. And although the word "existentialist" has been imported into this discussion from a later age, it is obvious that it was always possible to read the novel as the record of a failure.

It is interesting that we possess a critical essay on *Crime and Punishment* by the very Pisarev who held in real life the ferocious opinions maintained by Raskolnikov in his article. True to form, Pisarev sees Raskolnikov's progress away from those views as mere collapse, brought about by economic factors: "After committing the murder Raskolnikov conducts himself . . . like a petty cowardly and weak-nerved imposter for whom a major crime turned out to be beyond his strength." In our own time, the existentialist view, now firmly disengaged from the utilitarian, was forcibly maintained by Middleton Murry, in whose private moral hierarchy the criminal stands appreciably higher than the philanthropist; for example: "In the Underworld Raskolnikov had dreamed of committing crime for its own sake; in the waking world he was one of the thousands who do evil that good may come. He had never for one moment ventured outside the walls of the City of Good." "He was not even an unsuccessful criminal but an unsuccessful philanthropist." "Svidrigailov is the real hero of the book." "In Dostoevsky's eyes Raskolnikov could never have been more than an incomplete Svidrigailov." Criticism like this can be accused of much, but not, perhaps, of inconsistency.

I have said that Dostoevsky, if asked to choose between the two interpretations before us, would opt for the Christian one. Yet he could not do so without misgivings. The final account of the real relation between existential freedom and Christian love is never clearly set forth. Certainly they are intermittently opposed, and equally certainly at the crude level of plot the hero is lost by one party and gained by the other. But the metaphysical question is unsolved.

Take the case of Porfiry, the police investigator. Porfiry is not, like Svidrigailov, "above" philosophizing. Indeed, he gets pleasure from sharpening his formidable wits in metaphysical discussion (so different, as they say, from our English policemen). When Porfiry talks to Raskolnikov about the article on crime, he lays his finger at once on a weakness in Raskolnikov's case: Should there not be some external definition of the Exceptional Man, since otherwise some poor young fellow might think himself a Mahomet quite erroneously . . . ? The shaft is well-aimed, since this may well be Raskolnikov's situation. But at the same time, philosophically, a blow is struck for the utilitarian as opposed to the existentialist principle. We saw how the Underground Man confounded his utilitarian opponent by drawing away from under him all public means of defining pleasure. Without such means, vacuous caprice is supreme, and, as prediction becomes impossible, so justification in terms of ends and means becomes impracticable. Porfiry is thus gently forcing on Raskolnikov the necessity to choose between an arbitrary crime and one that is to be justified in terms of foreseeable consequences. With this question Porfiry strikes a shrewd blow for utilitarianism. Nor is it his last.

For Porfiry definition of one's role is necessary to every human being: "What you need more than anything in life is a definite position." This, as he presents it, is removed by only a hair's breadth from the existentialist position to which it is opposed. The existentialist finds a strange heroism in the resistance maintained by the free individual to encroaching definitions. But there could be no heroism in this if such freedom were not arduous, and such definitions insidiously comforting. Porfiry's case, in a way, consists of a strengthening of these adjectives. Individualist, predefinitional freedom is not just arduous, it is actually intolerable. Social definition is not just comforting, it is a psychological necessity. This is the foundation of his Socratic method. He attacks the criminal not with blows or proofs, but with the one really unbearable thing, uncertainty. Those Underground Men need only be fed to overflowing with the very indeterminacy they say they think so much of, and they will soon vomit up all their squalid crimes: "Have you seen a butterfly round a candle? That's how he will keep circling and circling round me. Freedom will lose its attractions." One thinks of the course taken by the later literature of existentialism. While a Meursault or a Roquentin may find a certain grim excitement in their supposedly undetermined worlds, it is left to Kafka to show what real indeterminacy does to man. Just as Joseph K in *The Trial* begins by arguing for his innocence but is soon desperate for conviction, so Raskolnikov is filled with fear by the thought that Porfiry thinks him *innocent*. We see Porfiry's technique at work in the superb rhetorical *occupatio* he plays upon Raskolnikov:

> Why, if I had the slightest suspicion of you, should I have acted like that? No, I should first have disarmed your suspicions and not let you see I knew of that fact, should have diverted your attention and suddenly dealt you a knock-down blow . . . saying: "And what were you doing, sir, pray, at ten or nearly eleven at the murdered woman's flat and why did you ring the bell and why did you ask about blood? And why did you invite the porters to go with you to the police-station, to

the lieutenant?" That's how I ought to have acted if I had a
grain of suspicion of you.

Here we see the weapon of uncertainty in the hands of a master.

At the same time Porfiry professes—but with no great enthusiasm—
certain fundamental notions of traditional Russian Christianity. Once
again his approach is that of the practical psychologist. Speaking of the
workman Nikolay, whose gratuitous "confession" sprang from some religious "need to suffer," Porfiry says, "Suffering, too, is a good thing. Suffer! Maybe Nikolay is right in wanting to suffer."

I think we may say that Dostoevsky hates Porfiry. It might be
thought that his commendation of suffering would redeem him in the eyes
of his creator. But Porfiry recommends suffering as a doctor might recom-
mend a dose of castor oil. And, more importantly, Dostoevsky's own attitude to suffering is not perhaps an unequivocal as it is often supposed to
be. People often speak of Dostoevsky as if his novels were solely taken up
with endless orgies of repentance, voluptuous agonies of remorse. Freud
in an essay dryly compared Dostoevsky with the barbarians of the great
migrations, who "murdered and did penance for it, till penance became an
actual technique for enabling murder to be done." But Raskolnikov finds
his new life without passing through any vale of contrition. The immemo-
rial pattern of self-prostration is rather part of the background "noise" of
the novel. It is the lesser characters, such as Marmeladov, who perform
this part. Whenever Raskolnikov attempts it, there is an effect of distor-
tion, something is false, the movement cannot be completed. To Sonia it
seems clear as day that if Raskolnikov has committed murder he must
"suffer and expiate" his sin, must "stand at the cross-roads, bow down,
first kiss the earth which you have defiled and then bow down to all the
world and say to all men aloud, 'I am a murderer!' Then God will send
you life again." God sent Raskolnikov life again, but not on such terms.
True, Raskolnikov does, in a sort of nervous spasm, kneel in the street,
but the words "I am a murderer" die on his lips.

This is surely the terrible honesty of the greatest art. Had Dostoevsky
been the theological sensationalist he is often described as being, here lay
his inevitable climax. But instead he breaks his climax; at the moment of
highest expectation everything seeps away into the earth, for no better reason than that anything else would be false. The hunched figure of Raskolnikov on his knees in the mud, utterly lacking the innocent dignity of Sonia, even of Marmeladov, spurious, but pitiably trying at last in the most
uncomprehending way to learn—this provides by a kind of deliberate pri-

vation of our appetites the most moving moment in the book. The way of prostration and submission is never to be Raskolnikov's.

Even after he has given himself up and is going to his voluntary imprisonment he jibs at all those round him who prate of his need for suffering. In the strangest way they recall Job's comforters in their easy rationalisation of things, and Raskolnikov becomes a Job-like figure in his very resistance to the facile pains held out on every side:

> "They say it is necessary for me to suffer! What is the object of these senseless sufferings? Shall I know any better what they are for, when I am crushed by hardships and idiocy, and weak as an old man after twenty years penal servitude?"

There is a spark of the old Raskolnikov in this, the Raskolnikov who told Sonia that the worst sin she had committed was the destruction of herself. Even if it were not obvious from the tone of the writing, we know from a fragment of external evidence that Dostoevsky was drawn at times to admire the rebel in Raskolnikov; in the manuscript of the novel he scribbled in the margin beside a passage showing just this side of Raskolnikov, "Damn it! That's true in part." Surely it evokes from the reader a deeper sympathy than is ever aroused by the self-crucifixion of a Marmeladov or even a Sonia. Sympathy, and also a kind of relief, like the relief we feel when, in reading the terrible self-lacerating sonnets of Gerard Manley Hopkins, we come upon the unfamiliar beauty of the lines

> My own heart let me more have pity on; let
> Me live to my sad self hereafter kind.

There is another kind of egotism than the utilitarian, with its own moral claim.

Before he leaves for Siberia Raskolnikov insists that he is not thinking of expiation, and in Siberia he persists in maintaining that his conscience is at rest. Of course in this he is wrong, and half-knows that he is wrong, of that there is no question. What is important is the manner of his correction.

This is done very quietly, without tear-floods or sigh-tempests, indeed with a miraculous simplicity. Raskolnikov falls ill in prison; during his convalescence, Sonia herself falls ill and is unable to visit him. Then, on a bright, warm day Raskolnikov is sitting looking at the river when he becomes aware that Sonia has come and sat down beside him. Quite suddenly he weeps and throws his arms round her knees; and the thing has happened. It may be said that this, precisely, is the moment of penitent self-prostration which I have been labouring to withhold from Raskolnikov. But if that is so, why does Raskolnikov make no reference to his crime? The kneeling of Marmeladov is essentially retrospective; it has unmistakable reference to what he has done. Raskolnikov's action, on the other hand, is obscurely prospective.

Roger L. Cox in his book on Shakespeare and Dostoevsky seeks to resolve this difficulty by applying to it knowledge gained from biblical scholarship. We must distinguish, he says, between Paul and John. In the Pauline epistles sin is conceived as a primordial hostile principle, prior to the individual fallen soul, to be defeated only by rebirth. But in John's Gospel, the sinner is not so much guilty as unhappy, cut off from *light;* sin is posterior to the individual, arising by mere consequence from his initial darkness, that is, his inability to see, believe and love. Paul sees morality in terms of creation, John in terms of revelation. That is why in Shakespeare's *King Lear,* where the morality is Pauline, Lear must be broken before he be remade, while in *Crime and Punishment,* where the morality is Johannine, Raskolnikov need only turn and look up.

It is an attractive thesis. It would seem that the Eastern Church has traditionally stressed John's Gospel where the Western Church has stressed the Pauline epistles. Moreover the most prominent scriptural reference in *Crime and Punishment,* that to Lazarus, is Johannine. Moreover the general movement of the book is from darkness to light, and from wretchedness to happiness. Lafcadio Hearn observed in 1885 that the mental sufferings of Raskolnikov "are not the sufferings of remorse, but of nervous affection." Somehow the shrewdness of this was always off-key. The reason is that although we do not find Pauline remorse, we do find, persistently, a moral element in Raskolnikov's unhappiness. Hearn wrote from an unconsciously Pauline standpoint: no remorse, no morality. The only conclusion available to him is that Raskolnikov's condition is merely pathological. But it has a further, Johannine dimension: he is a soul in darkness.

But although this account has so much to commend it, it is not completely satisfying. To begin with, the scriptural distinction is perhaps a little too neat. Five minutes with Cruden's *Concordance* is enough to show that Paul is as fond of "light" as John, and "regeneration" no less crucial to John than to Paul. This perhaps is sufficient ground for suspicion, at least. More importantly for our purpose, the substitution of the model of revelation for (re-)creation does not really explain why Raskolnikov should not clearly repent. Light and clarity, surely, should produce not oblivion but articulate acknowledgment. There must be some other impediment.

The truth is that Raskolnikov did what he did in the name of freedom, and neither he nor his creator can bring himself to call that wrong. Raskolnikov, though completely reconciled with Sonia at the end, never quite did things in the way she had wanted. And the suggestion seems to be that, in this, he was wiser than she. The implication that the murder was after all an authentic act of freedom, indefinable, *sui generis* and therefore not to be classified as any sort of sin, survives the conclusion of the book.

Clearly if some inalienable good persists in pure freedom, Dostoevsky is under very great pressure to claim that such freedom is compatible with—perhaps essential to—Christianity. The dim outline of a solution seems to rise before us: if the freedom of a Svidrigailov or a Stavrogin is devilish, might not there be another freedom, a baptised freedom, which God might love? After all, the notion that "everything is permitted" is not confined to the writing of modish freethinkers: remember, "All things are lawful unto me." These are the words of Paul to the Corinthians. It is certain that this thought beckoned Dostoevsky, since so much of his later work is a kind of quest for it.

It will be apparent from what I have just said that I do not believe that *Crime and Punishment,* for all its cogency of formal structure, demonstrates this baptised freedom. Further, even Dostoevsky's last great work, *The Brothers Karamazov,* in which a more sustained onslaught is made upon the problem, does not in my view attain to a solution. No solution is attained because none can be. Dostoevsky was too honest and too intelligent to delude himself in this matter. The example of Kierkegaard notwithstanding, existentialism is incompatible with Christianity. As long as freedom is conceived in existentialist terms it will resist any attempt to baptise it. To develop a notion of freedom as essentially rule-governed and hence both rational and moral—this would be a freedom Christianity could proudly display as one of the brightest jewels in its crown.

Philosophical Pro and Contra in Part 1 of *Crime and Punishment*

Robert Louis Jackson

> *I suffered these deeds more than I acted them.*
> SOPHOCLES, *Oedipus at Colonus*

The burden of part 1 of *Crime and Punishment* is the dialectic of consciousness in Raskolnikov. This dialectic propels him to crime and, in so doing, uncovers for the reader the motives that lead him to crime, motives deeply rooted in his character and in his efforts to come to terms with the necessities of his existence. Leo Tolstoy grasped the essence of the matter in "Why Men Stupefy Themselves" (1890), writing that Raskolnikov lived his "true life" not when he murdered the old pawnbroker and her sister and when he was living in a strange flat planning murder, but

> when he was not even thinking about the old woman, but lying on the sofa at home, deliberating not at all about the old woman and not even about whether it was permissible or not permissible at the will of one man to wipe off from the face of the earth an unnecessary and harmful person, but was deliberating about whether or not he ought to live in Petersburg, whether or not he ought to take money from his mother, and about other questions having no bearing at all on the old woman. And precisely at that time, in that region—quite independent of animal activities—the question of whether or not he would kill the old woman was decided.

If the fundamental matters or issues over which Raskolnikov deliberates are immediate and practical ones, his reponses to these matters have broad

From *The Art of Dostoevsky: Deliriums and Nocturnes.* © 1981 by Princeton University Press.

implications that have direct bearing on the crime. Here we may rightly speak of a moral-philosophical pro and contra.

Part 1 begins with Raskolnikov's test visit to the old pawnbroker and ends with the visit in which he murders the old lady and, incidentally, her sister Lizaveta. The murder itself is also, in a deeper sense, a test or experiment set up to determine whether he has the right to transgress. He starts out in a state of indecision or irresolution and ends with a decisive action—murder—an apparent resolution of his initial indecision. But does the murder really constitute a resolution of Raskolnikov's dialectic? Does he really "decide" to murder the pawnbroker? Or does not chance, rather, serve to mask his failure to decide with his whole being? Is he master or slave here?

The final line of part 1 alone suggests the answer: "Bits and fragments of some kind of thoughts swarmed about in his head, but he was unable to get hold of a single one of them, he could not concentrate upon a single one of them in spite of all his efforts." Raskolnikov's dialetic of consciousness continues to be dramatized in his thoughts, actions, and relationships after the murder (parts 2–6). It is only in the epilogue (chap. 2) that this dialectic is dissolved—not resolved—on a new, developing plane of consciousness. Raskolnikov's inability to focus his thoughts on anything, his inability consciously to resolve anything after his reconciliation with Sonya in the epilogue ("he was simply feeling") constitutes a qualitatively different state of consciousness from the chaos of mind he experienced right after the murder. These two moments of consciousness are in almost symmetrical opposition. The movement or shift from one to the other constitutes the movement in Raskolnikov's consciousness from hate (unfreedom) to love (freedom).

The movement from test to test, from rehearsal to experimental crime, from theory to practice, is marked by a constant struggle and debate on all levels of Raskolnikov's consciousness. Each episode—the meeting with Marmeladov and his family, Raskolnikov's reading of his mother's letter with its account of family affairs, his encounter with the drunken and bedraggled girl and the policeman, and his dream of the beating of the mare—is marked by a double movement: sympathy and disgust, attraction and recoil. Each episode attests to what has been called Raskolnikov's "moral maximalism." Yet each also attests to a deepening skepticism and despair on the part of Raskolnikov, a tragic tension toward crime in both a psychological and a philosophical sense.

The immediate issues of this pro and contra are nothing more or less than injustice and human suffering and the question of how a person shall respond to them. But the deeper evolving question—on which turns

Raskolnikov's ultimate response to this injustice and suffering—is a judgment of mankind: is man a morally viable creature or simply and irredeemably bad? Do man and the world make sense? Raskolnikov's murder of the old pawnbroker is the final expression of the movement of his dialectic toward a tragic judgment of man and society. The ideological concomitant of his paralysis of moral will (the scenes following his chance encounter on the street with Lizaveta) is a rationalistic humanism that is unable to come to terms with evil in human existence. Lacking larger spiritual dimensions, this ideology ends by postulating incoherence and chaos in man and his environment and, in turn, in a universe in which man is a victim of fate.

The stark realism and pathos of Marmeladov's and his family's life at first cools the hot and agitated Raskolnikov. The novel rises to its first epiphany in the tavern: out of the troubled posturing and grotesquerie of Marmeladov comes a mighty prose poem of love, compassion, and forgiveness (echoing Luke 7:36–50). It constitutes an antithesis to Raskolnikov's proud and rebellious anger. Raskolnikov visits the Marmeladovs, responds warmly to them, and leaves some money behind. But the scene of misery evokes incredulity and despair in him. If Marmeladov's "confession," which opens chapter 2, accents the central redemptive note in *Crime and Punishment,* the final lines of the chapter stress antithetical notes of despair and damnation. The sight of human degradation so overwhelms Raskolnikov that fundamental doubts about man and human nature are called forth in him. Stunned that people can live in this way, that indignity, vulgarity, and discord can become an accepted part of man's life, Raskolnikov explodes: "Man can get used to anything—the scoundrel!" These strange ruminations follow: "But what if man really isn't a *scoundrel,* man in general, I mean, the whole human race; if he is not, that means that all the rest is prejudice, just imaginary fears, and there are no barriers, and that is as it should be!" These lines are crucial in posing the underlying moral and philosophical issues of *Crime and Punishment.*

The motif of adaptation is heard throughout Dostoevsky's works— from *Poor Folk* through *House of the Dead* to *The Brothers Karamazov.* It attests, from one point of view, to human endurance, the will to survive. Yet from another view, it expresses a deeply tragic idea, implying that man will yield feebly to suffering, oppression, injustice, unfreedom, in short, to triumphant evil. Man in this conception is man as the Grand Inquisitor finds him: weak and vile. Such adaptation arouses only contempt in the rebellious Raskolnikov.

Raskolnikov's rebellion implies a positive standard or norm of human

behavior, morality, life. Merely to speak of man as a scoundrel for adapt-
ing to evil is to posit another ideal, to affirm by implication that man
ought not to yield weakly to degradation and evil. But the thought that
occurs to Raskolnikov at this point is one that links him directly with the
Grand Inquisitor. We may paraphrase it as follows: what if all this vile
adaptation to evil is not a deviation from a norm; that is, what if villainy
pure and simple is, ab ovo, the human condition? What if, as Raskolnikov
later puts it, every one of the people scurrying about on the streets "is a
scoundrel and predator by his very nature"? If such be the case, if man is
truly defective by nature, then all our moral systems, standards, injunctions, pejorative epithets (the word "scoundrel" itself) are senseless prejudices and imaginary fears. It follows that if human nature is, morally
speaking, an empty plain, then "there are no barriers"; all is permissible,
"and that is as it should be!"

Raskolnikov's intense moral concerns provide evidence that man is
not a scoundrel and predator by nature. And it is the idea of adaptation as
testimony to man's endurance and will to live that is ultimately accepted
by Raskolnikov. Thus, Raskolnikov, after an encounter with prostitutes
on the streets, declares that it would be better to live an eternity on a
"square yard of space" than to die: "To live and to live and to live! No
matter how you live, if only to live! How true that is! God, how true!
What a scoundrel man is!" "And he's a scoundrel who calls him a scoundrel for that," he added a minute later.

Svidrigailov, the character who comes closest to an embodiment of
the principle that all is permissible, also poses the question that Raskolnikov is deliberating, though more dispassionately and cynically. Defending
himself against the charges that he persecuted Dunya in his home, he observes:

> Now let's just assume, now, that I, too, am a man, *et nihil hu-
> manum* . . . in a word, that I am capable of being attracted and
> falling in love (which, of course, doesn't happen according to
> our own will), then everything can be explained in the most
> natural way. The whole question is: am I a monster or am I
> myself a victim? Well, and what if I am a victim?
>
> (part 4, chap. 1)

Barely concealed in Svidrigailov's jocular question is the issue of human
nature. The underlying ethical and philosophical import of his question—
"Am I a monster or am I myself a victim?"—is clear: does a consideration
of his acts—man's acts ("Just assume, now, that I, too, am a man")—fall

under the rubric of ethics or the laws of nature? Are we really responsible for our behavior? Are the morally pejorative epithets "monster" or "scoundrel" really in order? Are we not simply creatures of nature?

Svidrigailov, we note, likes to appeal to natural tendencies. Very much like the Marquis de Sade's alter egos Clement (*Justine,* 1791) or Dolmance (*La philosophie dans le boudoir,* 1795), he appeals to nature as a reason for disposing entirely of moral categories or judgment. "In this debauchery, at least, there is something constant, based even on nature, and not subject to fantasy," Svidrigailov remarks in his last conversation with Raskolnikov. Indeed, Svidrigailov's conception of man would appear to be wholly biological—"Now I pin all my hope on anatomy alone, by God!"—a point of view that certainly undercuts any concept of personal responsibility.

The concept *homo sum, et nihil humanum a me alienum puto* ("I am a man and nothing human is alien to me") was for Dostoevsky a profoundly moral concept, implying the obligation squarely to confront human reality. "Man on the surface of the earth does not have the right to turn away and ignore what is taking place on earth," he wrote in a letter in 1871, "and there are lofty *moral* reasons for this: *homo sum et nihil humanum . . .* etc." Svidrigailov, however, takes the concept as an apologia for doing whatever he pleases. To be a man, in his view, is to be open to all that is in nature, that *is,* to nature in himself; it is to be in the power of nature (if not to *be* nature) and therefore not to be responsible. But his hope for salvation through Dunya and his final suicide are evidence that his confidence in anatomy has its cracks and fissures. In the final analysis, then, even for Svidrigailov (though infinitely more so for Raskolnikov), the question, "monster or victim?"—is he morally responsible or free to commit all vilenesses?—is a fateful question. Posing this question, in Dostoevsky's view, distinguishes man, even the Svidrigailovs, from Sade's natural man.

The problem of human nature raised by Raskolnikov and Svidrigailov, and lived out in their life dramas, is expressed directly by Ivan Karamazov. Apropos of his belief that man is incapable of Christian love, Ivan observes: "The real issue is whether all this comes about because of bad elements in people's character or simply because that is their nature." Raskolnikov's pessimistic conjecture at the conclusion of chapter 2 (and, even more, the evidence of his dream in chapter 5) can be compared with Ivan's bitter judgment of man in his famous rebellion. It can be described as the opening, and dominant motif, in a prelude to murder. The whole of *Crime and Punishment* is an effort to refute this judgment of man, to provide an answer, through Raskolnikov himself, to this tragic conjecture. The action in part 1, however, is moved by the almost syllogistic logic of Raskolnikov's pessimistic supposition.

Chapter 2 of part 1 contains the extreme moral and philosophical polarities of the novel: affirmation of both the principle of love, compassion, and freedom (which will ultimately embrace Raskolnikov through Sonya) and the principle of hate, the pessimistic view of man as a scoundrel by nature, the projection of the idea that all is permissible. The events of this chapter bring Raskolnikov full circle from compassion to nihilistic rage. Exposed is that realm of underground, ambivalent consciousness where love is compounded of pain and hate, of frustrated love; where extreme compassion for suffering and the good is transmuted into a contempt for man; where that contempt, finally, signals despair with love and the good, and nourishes the urge for violence and the sick craving for power that is born not only from an acute sense of injustice but from a tragic feeling of real helplessness and irreversible humiliation.

Here is our first contact with the matrix of Raskolnikov's "theoretical" crime, with the responses that will find explicit formulation in Raskolnikov's article and arguments. Here is the protean core of those shifting, seemingly contradictory motives: the "idea of Rastignac" (altruistic, utilitarian crime), as Dostoevsky put it, and the idea of Napoleon (triumph over the "anthill," and so forth). Here we see how the raw material of social and psychological experience begins to generalize into a social and philosophical point of view—and ultimately, into those ideas of Raskolnikov's that will tragically act back again upon life and experience.

The same cyclical pattern we have noted in chapter 2 dominates chapter 3. The chapter opens on a subtle note that disputes the depressing and abstract conjectures of Raskolnikov. Natasya, the servant girl, brings him soup, chattering about food and about Raskolnikov's affairs. She is the epitome of a simplicity, warmth, and goodness that cannot be gainsaid. She is a kind of spiritual harbinger of Raskolnikov's mother, whose letter he receives. This letter, like Raskolnikov's encounter with Marmeladov and his family, evokes a picture of self-sacrificing people who are helpless before the evil in the world, before the Luzhins and Svidrigailovs. Raskolnikov begins reading the letter with a kiss ("he quickly raised it to his lips and kissed it"), but he ends it with "an angry, bilious, malignant smile" curling about his lips. The letter produces the same ugly sensations in him as the scene in the Marmeladov household, the same sympathy and compassion turning into rage and rebellion. Raskolnikov later goes out for a walk as though "drunk," his shapeless body reflecting his inner rage and distress. His initial readiness to protect a helpless girl from the attentions of a pursuing stranger on the street is replaced almost immediately by a sense of revulsion, a raging amoral anger. Starting out with a gesture of goodness, Raskolnikov characteristically ends by abandoning the girl to evil in a classical gesture of underground malice.

Raskolnikov's basic skepticism about man and human nature emerges in his reflections on his mother, his sister Dunya, and their critical situation. He comprehends the sacrifice his mother and sister make for him as an ascent to Golgotha but in bitterness casts them among the innocents, those "Schilleresque 'beautiful souls' " who wave the truth away, who would rather not admit the vile truth about man. Dunya, Raskolnikov realizes, is prepared to suppress her moral feelings for the one she loves, for him. He almost venomously rejects the idea of this sacrifice of her freedom, peace of mind, conscience. It is a rejection, of course, of the Christian spirit of sacrifice that he finds in Sonya as well as in Dunya. "Dear little Sonya, Sonya Marmeladov, eternal Sonya, while the world lasts! But this sacrifice, this sacrifice, have you taken the measure of your sacrifice, both of you? Have you really? Do you have the strength? Will it be of any use? Is it wise and reasonable?" Raskolnikov's choice of words is symptomatic of his ideological illness. To the impulses of the heart he opposes utility, scales, self-interest. And this, of course, is rich soil for the cultivation of ideas of utilitarian crime. The appeal of utilitarian ethics emerges from a despairing sense of the uselessness of all human striving for justice and truth, from a sense of the vileness of human nature and a conviction that "people won't change, and nobody can remake them, and it's not worth wasting the effort over it!"

Raskolnikov rightly understands that what he rejects (the principle of love and self-sacrifice) is eternal. He rejects it in part out of despair with evil. But he also rejects it in the name of a false principle of self-affirmation and "triumph over the whole anthill," a false principle of freedom: "And I know now, Sonya, that whoever is strong and self-confident in mind and spirit is their master!" Raskolnikov's rejection of his family's spirit of self-sacrifice reflects, at least in part, his own distance from Dostoevsky's concept of self-sacrifice and, chiefly, from the ideal of an authentic freedom that such a spirit of self-sacrifice implies.

Raskolnikov's powerful impulses to good and his high potential for self-sacrifice are short-circuited by a sense of overwhelming injustice and evil, of absurd imbalance in the scales of good and evil. In the face of the world's misery, the rapacious Svidrigailovs and Luzhins, the pitiful and loathsome spectacle of man-adapting, Raskolnikov rebels: "I don't want your sacrifice, Dunya, I don't want it, mother dear! It shall not be as long as I live, it shall not, shall not! I won't accept it!"

Dostoevsky uses the word "anguish" to express Raskolnikov's state of mind here. His rebellion, indeed, looks back on the revolt of the Underground Man and forward to Ivan Karamazov's rebellion against divine harmony (if it be based on the innocent suffering of children). Deeply responsive to human suffering, Ivan, in his indignation, returns to God his "ticket" to future harmony. Yet this same humanitarian revolt, with its despair in a meaningful universe, leads him unconsciously to sanction the murder of his father. This same ethical paradox lies at the root of Raskolnikov's crime. Starting out with love and compassion for the "eternal" Sonya and for Dunya and his mother, Raskolnikov ends up with a rejection of love and sacrifice and with a rage at evil—a rage that itself becomes disfigured and evil. This rage, ethically motivated in its origins, deforms Raskolnikov and accentuates in him the elements of sick pride and self-will.

In this state of mind, Raskolnikov's thought is led back to his projected crime. "It shall not come to that," he insists: he would be "robbing" his family; but what can he do? The letter from his mother exposes his helplessness in a realm that is dear to him, drives him onto the path of action. He must either act, he feels, or "obediently" accept his fate, strangle everything in himself, "renounce every right to act, to live and to love!" Suddenly a thought flashes through his mind. It is the "monstrous vision" (*bezobraznaia mechta*) of his crime, and it is now taking on "some new and terrifying, quite unfamiliar form." This new and threatening form is revealed to him in his "terrible dream" or nightmare in chapter 5: the beating and killing of the mare.

Raskolnikov's dream, echoing earlier incidents, situations, and emotional experiences, is a psychological metaphor in which we can distinguish the conflicting responses of Raskolnikov to his projected crime: his deep psychological complicity in, and yet moral recoil before, the crime. What has received less attention, however, is the way in which the underlying philosophical pro and contra are revealed in the separate elements of the dream (pastoral church and cemetery episode, tumultuous tavern, and mare-beating scene); how the scene of the beating itself, this picture of Russian man and reality, raises the central and grave question of part 1: what is the nature of man? In its oppressive realism, and in the pessimism of its commentary on man, this dream yields only to the tale "Akulka's Husband" in *House of the Dead*.

The opening recollection in Raskolnikov's dream, though darkened by an atmosphere of impending evil, embodies Dostoevsky's pure aesthetic-religious ideal. Sacred form, harmony, and reverence define the boy's first memory of the tranquil open landscape, the stone church with its green cupola, the icons, the simple rituals, the cemetery, and, finally, the tombs of his grandmother and younger brother, with their clear promise of resurrection. "He loved this church" and its atmosphere. In Raskolnikov's purified and almost completely submerged memory of sacred form, spirituality, and beauty, there lies the seed of Raskolnikov's own moral and spiritual renewal. But the path to the church and cemetery—to resurrection—goes by the tavern on the edge of town. Here he encounters the crowd of drunken, brawling peasants with their "drunken, fearsome, distorted faces" and their "shapeless and hoarse singing." Here everything is desecration and deformation. The faces of the people in Raskolnikov's nightmare tell the tale: this is a demonized universe. It created an "unpleasant impression" on the boy. On the deepest level of the dream, then, we may speak of the coexistence—passive, we shall see—of two barely contiguous worlds: the ideal world of Christianity, with its aesthetic-religious ideals, and the real world claimed by the devil.

But Raskolnikov dreams again. It is a holiday, a day of religious observance. The peasants, however, are drunk and in riotous spirits. There is an overloaded cart drawn by a poor mare. Suddenly, a crowd of peasants, shouting and singing, emerges from the tavern, "dead drunk, in red and blue blouses." At the invitation of the driver, Mikolka, they pile onto the cart, followed by a "fat, red-faced peasant woman" in a "red calico dress and beaded cap and high shoes; she was cracking nuts and laughing. In the crowd all around they're also laughing." Then the effort to start the cart and the brutal process of beating, and finally killing, the mare commences.

This terrible and terrifying scene is simultaneously a rehearsal for murder and a statement on man. "Don't look," the father tells the boy. But Dostoevsky forces the reader to look—at the beating, at the crowd, at himself ("Man on the surface of the earth does not have the right to turn away"). "My property!" the peasant Mikolka screams repeatedly in his drunken rage, as he violently smashes away at the mare. This is a scene of absolute evil. In it surface in a strange symbiosis what are for Dostoevsky the most predatory instincts in man: those of power, sensuality, and possessiveness. The message of "my property" is clear: the fact that he owns the mare releases him from all moral obligations, because it is *his* good that is involved. The use of the word *dobro* here—with the dual meaning, property-goods, and ethical good—subtly suggests the smashing of all moral norms or "barriers," the triumph of raw egoism over any moral imperative in human relations. "My property! What I want—I go ahead and do!" screams Mikolka. Akulka's husband in *House of the Dead* cries, "Whatever I want to do to all of you now, that's what I'm going to do, because I'm no longer in control of myself." The motif "all is permissible" permeates Raskolnikov's nightmare, as it does "Akulka's Husband" and Ivan's stories of the cruelties inflicted on children. These are grim statements on man.

In Raskolnikov's nightmare, others also participate in the orgy of violence, or watch passively from the sidelines, laugh, and enjoy the spectacle, or just go on cracking nuts. There are some voices of condemnation. But they are drowned out. Even an old man who shouts indignantly, "You've got a cross on you or something, you little devil?" becomes demonized himself. As he watches the mare vainly straining and stumbling about, he too bursts into laughter.

"Thank God, it's only a dream!" exclaims Raskolnikov. But the monstrous dream is drawn from Russian life. Reality, Dostoevsky liked to emphasize, was more fantastic than fiction. The mare-beating scene is the center of world evil. It is not surprising that at this moment, on the threshold of crime, Raskolnikov's soul is "in confusion and darkness."

Are the people who inhabit Raskolnikov's nightmare monsters or victims? Ivan's question—and it is really Raskolnikov's as well—is very much to the point here: "The real issue is whether all this comes about because of bad elements in people's character or simply because that is their nature." The terrible event at the center of Raskolnikov's nightmare provides a tragic answer to this question. And if human nature is a moral wasteland, then "there are no barriers, and that is as it should be!" Raskolnikov's social-philosophical conclusions, here embodied in the action of his own psychodrama, represent a precipitous movement toward murder.

Certainly, the fractured character of Raskolnikov's moral consciousness is revealed in this dream. The boy identifies with the suffering mare, with the victim, as Raskolnikov does initially in his various encounters in part 1. He is in anguish to the point of hysteria. He cries and screams and at the end puts his arm around the mare's, "dead, bloodstained muzzle, and kisses her, kisses her on the eyes, on the mouth." But, as in Raskolnikov's waking hours, anguish turns into rage, and the boy "suddenly leaps up and in a frenzy rushes at Mikolka with his little fists."

Mikolka is clearly the oppressor, the embodiment of the principle of self-will. He could easily stand in for types like the pawnbroker, Luzhin, or Svidrigailov—all vicious people exploiting and degrading innocent people like Dunya, Lizaveta, or Sonya, quiet timid creatures with gentle eyes like those of the mare. It is against these vicious people that Raskolnikov revolts. But in his revolt, he is himself transformed into a monstrous, shapeless Mikolka. He himself becomes the alien oppressor, exalted by a new morality that crushes the guilty and innocent alike. In the image of the child, Raskolnikov recoils from the horror that Raskolnikov the man contemplates. But in the image of Mikolka, Raskolnikov prefigures his own role as murderer. Raskolnikov's dream has often been described as revealing the last efforts of his moral conscience to resist the crime. And this is true. The dream is a battle; but it is a battle that is lost. On the philosophical plane, as a statement on man, the dream is the tragic finale to the pro and contra of part 1, the final smashing of barriers.

The dream also expresses a central paradox. Here is hell, or, in any case, the postfall world plunged into terrible evil. Yet the evil is witnessed and judged in the innocent, prefall, mentality of the child. The world of the "fathers"—the adaptors, objectively indifferent to good and evil—is discredited ("Come along, don't look . . . it's not our business"). Their Christianity (witness the old man) is shameful and frightening at best: Christian ethics dissolve into laughter, the enjoyment of suffering, a Sadean realm that Dostoevsky explored in *House of the Dead*. The Christian ethos is not in men's hearts. The church is out of town, literally—but also in a metaphorical sense. It is passive. The real, active tension in the nightmare—dramatic and ideological—is in the almost Quixote-like opposition of absolute innocence to absolute evil, the inflamed demonic violence and brutality of Mikolka to the pure, idyllic sensibility, goodness, and anguish of the child. But the child, though rightfully protesting cruelty and evil, is unable conceptually to integrate evil in his prefall universe. This is the essential problem, as Dostoevsky conceives it, of such types as Raskolnikov and Ivan. Idealists, humanists, they are unable, at root, to disencumber themselves of their utopian dreams, their insistence on the moral absolute. Raskolnikov, very much like his sister, is a chaste soul.

In the final analysis, what Dostoevsky finds missing in Raskolnikov is a calm, reconciling Christian attitude, an attitude that, while never yielding to evil, nonetheless, in ultimate terms, accepts it as part of God's universe, as cloaked in the mystery of God's truth. Such an outlook can be seen in Zosima in *The Brothers Karamazov*. Dostoevsky himself strained to achieve a reconciling Christian attitude, made his final conscious choice in this direction, and indeed gives clear evidence of this choice (Raskolnikov's ultimate choice, we must believe) in the prelude to the nightmare. Yet at the same time, he invested the child's suffering and rage with deep pathos and anguish. The child's pure nature is ill-equipped to cope with reality or even grasp the deeper coherence of life's processes. Yet it seems a cardinal feature of Dostoevsky's own outlook that all genuine moral feeling must arise from an open confrontation of the pure ideal with reality. Such a confrontation, on the plane of everyday life, may be unpleasant, disruptive, unrealistic, and even absurd. But as Ivan Karamazov observes to Alyosha, "absurdities are frightfully necessary on earth. The world rests on absurdities, and without them, perhaps, nothing would ever have taken place in it." In Raskolnikov's nightmare, only the pure vision of a child, only the sacred indignation of an unsullied soul, holds out any hope to the world that is all but damned.

"Freedom, freedom!" is Raskolnikov's predominant sensation after his nightmare. "He was free now from those spells, that sorcery, that enchantment, that delusion." The nightmare is catharsis, purgation, momentary relief. It is only a dream, yet it brings him face to face with himself. "Lord! is it really possible, really possible that I will actually take an ax, will hit her on the head, split open her skull . . . slip in the sticky warm blood?" he wonders. "Good Lord, is it really possible?" The day before, he recalls, he had recoiled from the idea of crime in sick horror. Now he remarks inwardly, and significantly: "Granted that everything decided upon this month is as clear as day, true as arithmetic. Lord! Yet I really know all the same I shall never come to a decision!" Indeed, Raskolnikov will never decide to commit the crime. He will never consciously, actively, and with his whole moral being choose to kill—or, the reverse, choose not to kill. His "moral resolution of the question" will never go deeper than "casuistry." And yet he will kill! He will lose his freedom (which in any case, after his nightmare, is deceptive) and be pulled into crime and murder—so it will seem to him—by some "unnatural power." Like Ivan Karamazov—but unlike Ivan's brother Dmitry—Raskolnikov will *allow* circumstances to shape his destiny.

Here a contrast with Dmitry is instructive. Dmitry spent the two days before the murder of his father (which he did not, in the end, commit) "literally casting himself in all directions, 'struggling with his fate and saving himself,' as he himself put it later." Dmitry's open, if naive, recognition of his opposing impulses and freedom to kill or not to kill, as well as his awareness of competing "philosophies" within him, is the crucial internal factor that helps to save him in the end from the crime of murder. Raskolnikov's dialectic of consciousness also constitutes a struggle, but his dialectic moves him toward, not away from, the crime. In the end, one philosophy triumphs: he loses his freedom (he blames the crime, significantly, on the devil) and yields to his obsession. Dmitry, on the other hand, triumphs over his obsession. Significantly, he attributes his victory to God.

Raskolnikov's deeply passive relationship to his crime often has been noted. Yet this passivity is not a purely psychological phenomenon. It is, Dostoevsky clearly indicates, closely linked with Raskolnikov's world view, an area of very intense activity for him. As Raskolnikov realizes later on, and as his own thinking and choice of language suggest, he is dominated at the time of the crime by a belief in fate, a general superstitious concern for all sorts of chthonic forces, perhaps even a taste for the occult (elements that, in Svidrigailov, have already surfaced in the form of ghosts). Dostoevsky alludes to Raskolnikov's problem directly in his notes to the novel. "That was an evil spirit: How otherwise could I have overcome all those difficulties?" Raskolnikov observes at one point. And a few lines later these significant lines: "I should have done that. (*There is no free will. Fatalism*)." And, finally, these crucial thoughts: "Now why has my life ended? Grumble: But God does not exist and so forth." Dostoevsky's own belief emerges even in these few notes: a loss of faith in God, or in the meaningfulness of God's universe, must end with the individual abandoning himself to a notion of fate.

Raskolnikov shares his proclivity toward fatalism with a number of Dostoevsky's heroes—for example, the Underground Man, the hero of "A Gentle Creature," and Aleksey Ivanovich in *The Gambler*. The similarities between Raskolnikov's and the gambler's problems are striking. Both men are dominated by a sterile, rationalistic outlook; both place themselves in a position of challenging fate; both lose their moral awareness in the essential act of challenge (murder, gambling); both seek through their acts to attain to an absolute freedom from the so-called laws of nature that are binding on ordinary men; both, in the end, conceive of themselves as victims of fate. Such types continually are seeking their cues or directives outside of themselves. Quite symptomatic, in this connection, is Raskolnikov's prayerful remark after his dream: "O Lord!" he prayed, "show me my path, and I will renounce this cursed dream of mine!"

The fateful circumstance that strikes Raskolnikov "almost to the point of superstition" and that seems a "predestination of his fate" is his chance meeting with Lizaveta, a meeting that, in Raskolnikov's view, sets into motion the machinery of fate. Raskolnikov returns home after that meeting "like a man condemned to death. He had not reasoned anything out, he was quite incapable of reasoning; but suddenly he felt with all his being that he no longer had any freedom to reason or any will, and that everything suddenly had been decided once and for all." Similarly, he responds to a conversation he overhears in a restaurant—by "coincidence" two men give expression to "precisely the same thoughts" that had been cropping up in his own mind—as constituting "some kind of prefiguration, a sign":

> This last day which had begun so unexpectedly and had decided everything at once, had affected him in an almost completely mechanical way, as though somebody had taken him by the hand and were drawing him after him, irresistibly, blindly, with unnatural force, without objection on his part; as though a piece of his clothing had got caught in the wheel of a machine and had begun to draw him into it.
>
> (part 1, chap. 6)

Dostoevsky is not projecting an "accident" theory of personal history; but neither does he deny the role of chance. Chance is the eternal given. Without it there would be no freedom. Raskolnikov's encounter with Lizaveta was accidental (though not pure accident), and it was by chance that he overheard the conversation in which he recognized his own thoughts (although, as Dostoevsky wrote in his letter to M. N. Katkov on the novel, the ideas that infect Raskolnikov "are floating about in the air"). But these chance elements only set into motion a course of action that was seeking to be born, albeit without the full sanction of moral self.

What is crucial in Raskolnikov's situation is not so much the factor of chance as *his disposition to be guided by chance,* his readiness, as it were, to gamble, to seek out and acknowledge in chance his so-called fate. What is crucial to his action is the general state of consciousness that he brings to the moment of critical accident; and consciousness here is not only his nervous, overwrought state but the way he conceives of his relationship to the world. Such is the background of Tolstoy's keen perception that Raskolnikov's true existence and true moment of decision occurred not when he met the sister of the old lady, not when he was "acting like a machine," but when he was "only thinking, when his consciousness alone was working and when in that consciousness barely perceptible changes were taking place"—in realms affecting the total scope of his existence.

Raskolnikov seizes upon the various chance incidents that precede the murder as the action of fate, but he does not recognize that fate here has all the iron logic of his own inner fatality. His passivity—that state of drift in which he evades the necessity of choice and abandons all moral responsibility—is motivated, then, not only by his deep and unresolved moral conflicts but by a muddled rationalistic, fatalistic outlook that itself denies freedom of choice or moral responsibility, an outlook that in the end posits an incoherent universe. This outlook is not something that Raskolnikov merely picked up in reading or table talk. The sense of a blind, meaningless universe, of a loveless world dominated by an evil spirit—and this is conveyed in part 1—emerges from Raskolnikov's confrontation with the concrete social reality of Russian life, with the tragedy of its lower depths: its hopeless poverty, its degradation, its desolation. It is this confrontation with the human condition that violates the purity of Raskolnikov's ideal, that ruptures his faith in moral law and human nature, that bends him toward a tragic view of man and toward the view of a universe ruled by blind fate. It is this confrontation, in which compassion and contempt for man form an intimate dialectic, that nourishes the related structures of his ideas or ideology: his altruistic utilitarian ethics and his Napoleonic self-exaltation and contempt for the "herd." It is this confrontation that underlies his murder of the old pawnbroker.

Consciousness, of course, is not passive here. Raskolnikov, half-deranged in the isolation and darknes of his incomprehensible universe (the model of which is his little coffinlike room), actively reaches out into "history," into his loveless universe, to rationalize his own responses to reality and his own psychological needs. He is an intellectual. His ideas, moreover, acquire a dynamic of their own, raise him to new levels of abstraction and fantasy, and provide him, finally, with a theoretical framework and justification for crime. Yet whatever the independence of these ideas, as we find them in his article or circulating freely in taverns and restaurants, they acquire their vitality only insofar as they mediate the confrontation between individual consciousness and social reality, only insofar as they give expression to Raskolnikov's intimate social and psychological experience and his deepest organic responses to the world about him.

In one of his notebooks, as we have noted earlier, Dostoevsky prided himself as being the first writer to focus on

> the tragedy of the underground, consisting of suffering, self-punishment, the consciousness of something better and the impossibility of achieving that something, and, chiefly, consisting in the clear conviction of these unhappy people that all are alike and hence it is not even worth trying to improve. Consolation, faith? There is consolation from no one, faith in no one. But another step from here and one finds depravity, crime (murder). Mystery.

The profoundly responsive Raskolnikov, we might say, voluntarily takes on himself this tragedy of the underground. He experiences it internally, morally, in all its aspects and agonizing contradictions. His final step should have been love—a step toward humanity. Instead, experiencing the tragedy of life too deeply, and drawing from that tragedy the most extreme social and philosophical conclusions, Raskolnikov (a victim of his own solitude, ratiocination, and casuistry) takes a step away from humanity into crime, murder, mystery.

Such is the practical denouement of the philosophical pro and contra—the dialectic of consciousness of Raskolnikov—in part 1 of *Crime and Punishment*.

The Causes of Crime and the Meaning of Law: *Crime and Punishment* and Contemporary Radical Thought

Derek Offord

It is one of the qualities of the greatest writers of imaginative literature that they succeed in capturing in their works both what is of lasting, universal significance and what is of most pressing concern in their own age and for their own nation. They deepen our knowledge both of man's experience in general and of his condition in a given society in particular. Thus Turgenev, in *Fathers and Children,* the novel generally acclaimed as his masterpiece, recorded in the most topical terms a conflict between generations and classes which has a relevance far beyond the Russia of the 1860s. Similar praise may be accorded to Dostoevsky. His works have a profound bearing on some of the philosophical doctrines and political systems of the twentieth-century world and on the psychological condition of the individual in modern urban societies. They also throw light on problems such as crime, so central in Dostoevsky's major fiction, which have come increasingly to disturb those societies. There is much in his works, for example, that is portentous for a world in which antisocial behaviour often constitutes a pastime for the reasonably well-to-do rather than a matter of economic necessity for the destitute, and in which, perhaps even more importantly, indiscriminate violence is often accepted as a legitimate means to a supposedly worthy end. And yet the insights into these problems with which Dostoevsky can furnish us are the product of his participation in a debate about issues of great local and contemporary importance at the time when his novels were written. It is the relationship of *Crime and Punishment* to this debate that this [essay] is intended primarily to discuss.

From *New Essays on Dostoevsky,* edited by Malcolm V. Jones and Garth M. Terry.
© 1983 by Cambridge University Press.

II

Dostoevsky, when he came to write *Crime and Punishment* in 1865, had already made an extensive contribution, both in publicism and in imaginative literature, to the vigorous intellectual life of those years following the Crimean War and the death of Nicholas I when a more liberal regime flowered briefly in Russia and when the old order began to undergo irreversible change. In particular the hostility towards the radical camp which found expression in Dostoevsky's writing in the early sixties was to become one of the prime creative influences in his major fiction.

The radical camp, of course, contained individuals with divergent opinions. Moreover, the Western thinkers from whom the Russian radicals derived their convictions were themselves numerous and of varied complexion, ranging from the English utilitarian Jeremy Bentham, the early Welsh socialist Robert Owen, French utopian socialists such as Fourier, Cabet and Considérant, and the positivist Comte, to German philosophers and thinkers such as Feuerbach and L. Büchner, the contemporary English historian Buckle, scientists such as Darwin and popularizers of scientific thought, such as G. H. Lewes. But it is probably not grossly inaccurate to suggest that what was of most interest in Western thought to the Russian radicals of the sixties, and what constituted for Dostoevsky a core against which his creative energies should be directed, might be reduced to a fairly limited number of propositions which were given wide currency in the journal *Contemporary* and in the voluminous, wordy and extremely influential writings of Chernyshevsky in particular.

These propositions may be summarized as follows: firstly, that "no dualism is to be seen in man," that is to say man does not possess a spiritual dimension which is qualitatively different from his physical being; secondly, that man is governed by self-interest; thirdly, that he is at the same time a rational creature; fourthly, that he may therefore be made to see where his best interest lies and to act accordingly; fifthly, that since man is amenable to rational persuasion and since his best interest lies in cooperation with his fellows, one might realistically hope to construct in theory and then in practice a perfectly ordered society; sixthly, that the good is that which is useful, and the useful, for the radical "men of the sixties," was in turn that which promoted the dissemination and acceptance of the preceding propositions; and finally, that a scientific method of enquiry, and only that method of enquiry (with the help of which all the preceding propositions were supposedly formulated), could be applied successfully and profitably to the examination of human conduct, society and government.

Dostoevsky disagrees profoundly with every one of these propositions. In his first major novel, *Crime and Punishment,* he makes explicit or oblique references, which are caustic in their context, to thinkers who defend them, and vigorously disputes the propositions themselves. He implies, for example, that it is resurrection of the spiritual side of Raskolnikov's being which offers him his only hope of salvation after he has taken other lives. Furthermore, it is love of others, as preached and practised by Sonya, rather than love of self, which makes possible such regeneration. Raskolnikov is not capable of consistently rational conduct. His behaviour is frequently self-destructive. And Razumikhin inveighs bitterly against the socialist utopia (part 3, chap. 5). But in particular Dostoevsky sets out to test in his novel the strength and acceptability of the last two propositions of the radicals, which concern the equation of the good with the useful and the omnicompetence of the scientific method of enquiry. And it is through his examination of the subjects of the causes of crime and the nature and status of law that Dostoevsky explores the implications of these two propositions and concentrates his argument against those who defend them.

III

There are no doubt several reasons for Dostoevsky's choice of the subjects of crime and the law as his ground on which to do battle with the radicals.

Firstly, legal questions very much preoccupied educated people in Russia in the early 1860s and the novelist of the time, with his interest in contemporary reality, was entitled to devote attention to them. Overhaul of the judicial system was one aspect of the great reforms planned and carried out in Russia in the late 1850s and early 1860s. An ukase of 1864 finally provided for the establishment of new courts on the Western model. Numerous foreign books on jurisprudence were translated, published and reviewed in this period and the journals devoted much attention to legal questions. Dostoevsky's own journal *Epoch,* for example, carried lengthy articles on legal procedure, punishments, criminal law and lawyers, as well as the memoirs of an investigator, in the course of 1864–65. In 1865 Dostoevsky himself was contemplating an article on the courts, some notes for which are preserved in one of his notebooks. Thus references to changes in the law and its administration, the proliferation of the legal profession, litigation, the increase in crime—there are allusions to forgery, seduction and poisoning, as well as description of Raskolnikov's murders, in *Crime and Punishment*—help on one level to provide a broad social backcloth for the novel's main action.

Secondly, on a deeper level, the mentality of the criminal was a subject that already absorbed Dostoevsky, the novelist of profound psychological insight. He had intimate knowledge of the criminal, gained in his
years in prison among hardened convicts and recorded in *Notes from the
House of the Dead*. In the journal *Time,* which he had edited from 1861 to
1863, there had appeared transcripts of famous trials of the century, and
Dostoevsky himself had written a preface to the first transcript, dealing
with the trial of the French professional criminal Lacenaire, a murderer
who exhibits striking similarities to Raskolnikov (both Lacenaire and
Raskolnikov are educated but impoverished young men driven obsessively
to dominate; both are influenced by Napoleon, atheistic, antisocial and
vengeful; and both publish speculative articles. Raskolnikov on crime and
Lacenaire on the penal system). It may also be that the great fictional possi-
bilities of the subject of crime and its detection were underlined for Dostoevsky by the novels of Dickens, in so many of which crime, including
murder, is a central feature.

Thirdly, on the polemical level, the question of crime was one which
also preoccupied the socialists with whom Dostoevsky was taking issue.
Like their Western European mentors, the Russian radicals of the 1860s
expressed deterministic views on the causes of crime which seemed to
Dostoevsky as oversimplified as their views on the nature of man and his
society. Robert Owen—whom Chernyshevsky's hero, Lopukhov, describes as a "holy old man" and whose portrait hangs in Lopukhov's
room—had taught the Russian radicals that crime was a natural product of
the irrational organization of the British society of his day. The "poor and
uneducated profligate among the working classes," he wrote in his *New
View of Society,* "are now trained to commit crimes"; but with man's natural progression from a "state of ignorance to intelligence," and the consequent implementation of "rational plans for the education and general formation" of a society's members, crime would be eradicated. "Withdraw
these circumstances which tend to create crime in the human character,"
he wrote with the ingenuous benevolence of the early socialists, "and
crime will not be created," for the "worst formed disposition, short of
incurable insanity," would not long resist a "firm, determined, well-
directed, persevering kindness." Similarly, Büchner, who in the late fifties
and early sixties exercised an influence on the Russian radical intelligentsia
out of all proportion to his importance in the history of European thought,
argued in *Kraft und Stoff*—a work much admired, incidentally, by Bazarov—that the "chief causes of crime" were "deficiency of intellect, poverty and want of education." In the Russia of the 1860s, where it became

customary to explain a man's behaviour deterministically, as a product of his environment, views such as these were commonplace. Chernyshevsky, for example, in his major profession of faith, the article on the "anthropological principle in philosophy" asserted:

> After the need to breathe . . . man's most pressing need is to eat and drink. Very often, very many people lack the where-withal for the proper satisfaction of this need, and this lack is the source of the greatest number of all bad actions, of almost all situations and institutions which are constant causes of bad actions. If one were to remove this cause of evil alone, at least nine tenths of all that is bad would quickly disappear from human society: the number of crimes would decrease ten times.

Likewise Dobrolyubov stated, in the tortuous style characteristic of the radical publicism of the time, that "any crime is not a consequence of man's nature, but a consequence of the abnormal relationship to society in which he is placed."

Dostoevsky's antagonism to such views is a major source of tension in *Crime and Punishment*.

IV

Now it is one of the qualities of Dostoevsky as a novelist that he seems rarely to come down decisively in his works of art on the side of those views which it is clear from his publicistic works that he wished to promote. His vision as an artist is too complex to permit him to be one-sided or tendentious. It is arguable, for example, that he failed adequately to rebut the arguments of Ivan Karamazov against acceptance of God's world, although he himself evidently needed to disbelieve them. And by emphasizing the loathsomeness of the pawnbroker Alyona and the exploit-ative Luzhin he sets up persuasive arguments in *Crime and Punishment* in favour of the crime whose moral inadmissibility he undoubtedly hoped eventually to demonstrate.

Similarly he does not simply reject out of hand the radicals' thesis that poverty was a possible cause of crime (or at least a cause of the derange-ment which might induce it). On the contrary, he points out on the very first page of the novel that Raskolnikov was "crushed by poverty"; for the second day running, we read shortly afterwards, he had eaten virtually nothing, and clearly his debility and illness are related. The oppressive and stinking milieu, moreover, "jarred the young man's nerves which were al-

ready disturbed without that" (part 1, chap. 1). And when Raskolnikov
does refresh himself after his first visit to Alyona's, his thoughts clear and
all that has been passing through his mind suddenly seems nonsense, the
result of physical disorder (part 1, chap. 1). Furthermore, the view that
crime and social conditions are related is openly advanced in those chapters
of the novel in which characters, with the murder of Alyona and Lizaveta
in mind, debate the causes of crime. Luzhin, trying to restore his rapidly
dwindling credit when he visits Raskolnikov in part 2, delivers himself of
a disquisition on the growth of crime in Russia, a phenomenon which
Zosimov attributes to the fact that there have been "many economic
changes" (part 2, chap. 5). Later, during Raskolnikov's first visit to Porfiry, Razumikhin refers to a heated debate that had taken place the night
before, in which someone had expressed the view of the "socialists" that
"crime is a protest against the abnormality of the social order—and only
that, and nothing more, and no other causes are admitted." According to
this view "all crimes" would disappear once society was organized "normally" (part 3, chap. 5). It is a view which even Porfiry appears to en-
dorse: " 'environment' means a lot in crime," he affirms. And he seems
prepared to carry it to the extreme, since when Razumikhin asks him
whether "environment" could be said to explain the seduction of a ten-
year-old girl by a forty-year-old man, he replies "with surprising gravity":
"Well, in a strict sense it very probably is environment, even a crime committed against a little girl may very well be explained by 'environment' "
(part 3, chap. 5). Lebezyatnikov argues with even more conviction in favour of such social determinism. He believes that everything depends on
man's "surroundings" and "environment." "All on the environment," he
says in his broken Russian, "and man himself is nothing" (part 5, chap.
1). In the society of the future, therefore, when all is rationally arranged
in the interests of equality, there will not even be any fights.

However, we are not expected to accept the deterministic view of
man's behaviour and of the incidence of crime uncritically. We are put on
our guard against it by the fact that its advocates are, in Dostoevsky's
terms, unreliable. Zosimov, for example, merely voices the common-
places fashionable among the younger generation. As a doctor he is the
novel's main practitioner of the exact sciences which that generation exalted. He is the target of the invective of Razumikhin—the physically and
spiritually healthy foil to the sickly Raskolnikov—against the "dumb pro-
gressives" who understand nothing and show disrespect for man because
they take too narrow a view of him (part 2, chap. 4). And in practice Zosimov's judgement is repeatedly at fault: for instance he mistakenly assumes

the murderer to be an experienced criminal (part 2, chap. 5); he wrongly predicts that the arrival of Raskolnikov's mother and sister will have a beneficial effect on Raskolnikov (part 3, chap. 1); and he fails to see in what way Luzhin is a bad suitor for Dunya (part 3, chap. 2). As for Lebezyatnikov, he is discredited morally—he beats Katerina Marmeladova (part 1, chap. 2)—and intellectually—he is the main apostle of Western rationalism in the novel but has great difficulty in talking coherently in his native language (part 5, chap. 3). And Porfiry, although he is by no means an object of Dostoevsky's criticism, does have a notorious capacity to mislead others for his own ends (part 3, chap. 5). On the other hand Razumikhin, the most vehement opponent of the view that "crime is a protest against the abnormality of the social order," and "nothing more" (part 3, chap. 5), is the champion of values close to Dostoevsky's own. Indeed in a sense he is the "positive hero" of the novel, Dostoevsky's fictional response to the hero of Chernyshevsky's *What Is to Be Done?*, Rakhmetov, with whom Dostoevsky even confuses him at one point in a rough draft for one of the scenes of *Crime and Punishment*. Like Rakhmetov, Razumikhin is physically strong, resourceful, independent, strong-willed and solicitous for his friends. He too is capable of feats of great endurance: Rakhmetov lies on a bed of nails to strengthen his will; Razumikhin has gone through a whole winter without heating his room (part 1, chap. 4).

More importantly, besides casting doubt on the reliability of those who uphold the deterministic explanation of crime or appear to do so, Dostoevsky underlines the limitations of the explanation itself by demonstrating—as was habitual with him—that the problem could be approached from the opposite angle. The radicals' hatred of existing society and their overriding desire to bring about its material transformation lead them to attribute even individual acts of wrongdoing to unsatisfactory social conditions. Dostoevsky, on the other hand, being concerned above all with the spiritual condition of the individual, seeks to direct the attention of those who would examine the incidence of crime in a given society not so much to any aspects of the material environment as to those psychological factors which allow the individual to commit crime or fail to prevent him from doing so. Thus in *Crime and Punishment* he is perhaps less interested in motives for murder, such as the desire of the impoverished Raskolnikov to "get rich quick" (part 1, chap. 3), than in the modern attitudes which appear to make it irrational for him not to kill, given the weakening or absence of conscience. In particular he has in mind the utilitarian morality of the radicals who, in the course of their endeavours to redefine concepts and transform values associated with the established order, described the good as that which was useful and the greatest good as that which was useful to the greatest number, and commended the moral doctrine which they designated "rational and egoism."

As critics have frequently pointed out, Dostoevsky emphasizes the prevalence of the utilitarian morality of the radicals and makes clear its bearing on the murder which Raskolnikov commits. In the letter to his prospective publisher Katkov, which he drafted in September 1865 when *Crime and Punishment* was taking shape in his mind, Dostoevsky associated his hero's crime with current theories: the action was to take place in that year and the hero, who was to be a "man of the new generation," had been carried away by certain badly thought out ideas which were "in the air." Moreover, in order to emphasize that conversations about the possibility of killing in the interests of public utility were commonplace among the young generation, Dostoevsky has Raskolnikov overhear a student advancing *"exactly the same ideas"* as those he himself is pondering (part 1, chap. 6). (It is significant too that these ideas are put forward by a student, for it was in the higher educational institutions that the radicals found their most enthusiastic support.) Again, Porfiry emphasizes that the murder of the pawnbroker is a "modern" crime and that the murderer killed "in accordance with theory" (part 6, chap. 2).

But how precisely does the ascendancy of the new morality account for the commission of crimes which the proponents of that morality would attribute to social deprivation? The morality of the radicals, Dostoevsky seems to argue, may produce such destructive results in three ways. Firstly, the adoption of utility as the criterion by which to judge the value of actions makes for a blurring of distinctions between acts which are absolutely right and acts which are absolutely wrong, that is, right or wrong, moral or immoral, in all circumstances. Judgement of the quality of an action becomes dependent on extrinsic factors such as the value of its probable consequences. Seen from this point of view, acts which have traditionally appeared to be immoral are no longer necessarily held to be so. Lebezyatnikov exhibits this relativistic attitude when he says that what in the present society is "stupid" may in the rationally ordered society of the future be "intelligent" (part 5, chap. 1). But more importantly Raskolnikov himself applies it to crime. The murder, when its advantages have been calculated and the sum of its disadvantages subtracted, seems a useful act and is therefore " 'not a crime' " (part 1, chap. 6).

Secondly, by asserting the preeminence of the greatest number, utilitarianism tends to reduce individual human beings to mere ciphers who have value not so much in themselves as in relation to the larger groups to which they belong. It was not difficult to decide, Chernyshevsky wrote, on whose side "theoretical justice" lay: the interests of mankind in general stood higher than the advantage of an individual nation, the general interest of a whole nation stood higher than the advantage of a single class, and the interest of a numerous class stood higher than that of a numerically inconsiderable group. This "theoretical justice" had about it an inflexible quality which precluded appeal by the minorities or individuals who might be the victims of its implementation; it represented merely an "application of geometrical axioms" such as the " 'whole is greater than part of it.' " Likewise for Dostoevsky's student in part 1 of *Crime and Punishment* "justice" consists in the promotion of the interests of the many at the expense of the pawnbroker and may be expressed simply and indisputably in the form of an equation: "What do you think, wouldn't one tiny little crime be cancelled out by thousands of good deeds? For one life—thousands of lives, saved from rotting and decay. One death and a hundred lives in exchange—why it's arithmetic, isn't it?" (part 1, chap. 6).

Thirdly, by their doctrine of "rational egoism"—in which the Russian utilitarianism of the 1860s chiefly found expression—the radicals tended to vindicate *egoistic* actions if the consequences of those actions could be claimed to have general utility. In this doctrine—which appears oddly incompatible with the socialist convictions it was supposed to bolster—the radicals contrived to accommodate both the proposition that man was governed by self-interest and belief in the feasibility of a utopia based on cooperation, by maintaining that man, when properly enlightened, would derive his selfish pleasure from performing acts of general utility. Raskolnikov clearly finds justification for his crime in the doctrine's identification of pursuit of personal profit, on the one hand, and promotion of general wellbeing, on the other (even though later, when he hears Luzhin parrot the doctrine, he is repelled by this potentiality in it [part 2, chap. 5]). For Raskolnikov seems to believe, as it was Dostoevsky's intention that he should, that the murder of the pawnbroker and the theft of her money would benefit both himself and others: it would alleviate his own poverty but would also liberate his exploited sister from Luzhin and rid society of a louse.

Thus the radicals, far from providing a correct explanation of the incidence of crime in society, are putting forward moral views which are themselves responsible for crime's growth. The establishment of their doctrines, whose apparently incontestable veracity seemed to Chernyshevsky to preclude any "unsteadiness in convictions," has in the view of Dostoevsky and those who were likeminded had the opposite effect: it has actually produced a discernible "unsteadiness in the moral order." And far from tending to hasten the advent of a utopia in which acts hitherto considered criminal cease to be perpetrated, these doctrines encourage the development of an anarchic society in which such acts merely cease to be considered criminal and therefore may proliferate.

V

From the early stages of *Crime and Punishment* Dostoevsky puts forward implicit arguments against the acceptability and even against the practicability of the utilitarian rationalization of crime. In the first place Raskolnikov himself tends to criticize rationalistic thinking when those he loves are the victims of its application. He is infuriated, for example, at the prospect of statisticians treating his sister as merely a number in a table indicating the percentage of the population which turns to prostitution each year (part 1, chap. 4). In the second place, there are strong indications that human behaviour is not so exclusively rational as the utilitarians believe: Raskolnikov's crime is logically planned—he even measures the distance ("exactly 730" paces [part 1, chap. 1]) between his lodging and the pawnbroker's—and yet over its actual commission his reason has very little control. (Indeed he is forced to commit another murder, the need for which he had planned to obviate by ensuring that Lizaveta would not be at home.) Moreover, the deliberate artistic confusion of the first part of the novel, with its disjointed time sequence and sometimes fractured style, serves to point up the disorientation of the character to whom issues seem in theory to be so clearcut. But although these factors serve from the beginning to undermine the value of the morality Raskolnikov has adopted, in fact the search for a sound explanation of his crime leads deeper into error. For the theories which Dostoevsky has Raskolnikov express in part 3 of the novel, concerning the right of certain individuals to "cross over" normal moral boundaries and to commit acts generally deemed criminal, represent an examination of some of the further implications of the new outlook. Whereas the first apparent explanation of the murder raises the question of how an act should be judged and affirms that its utility should be calculated, the second explanation raises the question as to who should make that judgement and calculation.

Commentators have drawn attention to the relationship between, on the one hand, the ideas Raskolnikov expresses in part 3 of the novel, and, on the other, those advanced in a book by Napoleon III and in the works of certain Russian radicals who wrote for the journal *Russian Word* and were by 1865 conducting an acrimonious polemic with the epigones of Chernyshevsky on *Contemporary*. It has also been noted that the use of the word *raskol,* chosen by Dostoevsky to denote the schism in the radical intelligentsia in the title of an article published in 1864 in his journal *Epoch* (which on more than one occasion mentioned the disagreements among the radicals with evident satisfaction), would seem to anticipate the name, Raskolnikov, chosen by him for the hero of the novel he began to write in the following year. And, of course, Lebezyatnikov refers obliquely to this schism in the novel itself (part 5, chap. 1). But since a few very striking similarities between the views expressed in *Russian Word* and those of Raskolnikov have not been fully brought out, it is worth briefly glancing again at this polemic and at the writings of Pisarev in particular.

In many respects Pisarev's views coincide with Chernyshevsky's. Pisarev preaches a materialistic doctrine similar to Chernyshevsky's; he believes that man is governed by self-interest; he repeatedly upholds the view that it is profitable for the individual to behave in socially useful ways; and he writes an extended encomium to the new men who practise this doctrine and whom Chernyshevsky had portrayed in his novel *What Is to Be Done?* But Pisarev's rebellion is altogether more iconoclastic than Chernyshevsky's. Whereas Chernyshevsky, writing in 1855 as the old order was just beginning to weaken, had given the cautious title *Aesthetic Relations of Art to Reality* to the dissertation in which he called in question the old belief that the beautiful was superior to everyday reality, Pisarev, writing in 1865, when the attack on the old order was well advanced, undertook nothing less than a "destruction" (*razrusheniye*) of aesthetics. Old barriers were to be torn down unceremoniously. Literature, Pisarev wrote in 1861, for example, should strive to emancipate man "from the various constraints imposed on him by the timidity of his own thought, by caste prejudice, by the authority of tradition, by the striving towards a common ideal and by all the obsolete lumber that prevents a living man from breathing freely and developing in every direction." His readers were exhorted to try to "live a full life," without stifling what was *original* in them in order to accommodate the established order and the taste of the crowd. He urged the destruction, together with other old values, of that "artificial system of morality" which crushed people from the cradle. In short, Pisarev's doctrines are partially similar to those of Chernyshevsky; but, as Dostoevsky jotted in his notebooks, probably under the impression of the article from which I have quoted, "Pisarev has gone further." In *Crime and Punishment* Lebezyatnikov, claiming that he would argue even with Dobrolyubov were he to rise from his grave, makes the same point in similar terms. "We have gone further in our convictions," he says, identifying himself with Pisarev and his supporters. "We reject more" (part 5, chap. 1).

Now it very often happened that ideas being expressed in the Russian publicism of the age were embodied in the fiction and that the fiction in turn stimulated the publicism. In fact between the publicism and the fiction there existed an intimate relationship; they responded to one another and moved forward together dialectically. And the freedom from traditional restraints already being advocated by Pisarev in 1861 found its fictional representation in Bazarov, the literary prototype of the new man to whom Turgenev applied the title "nihilist." Pisarev was delighted to accept Bazarov as an example for the new generation to follow, although in the second of the two substantial tracts he devoted to examination of Turgenev's novel he preferred the name "realist." The mission of the new man, as Bazarov saw it, was not to build but to destroy what impeded new construction, "to clear space," and Pisarev gleefully proceeded to elaborate on the freedom the destroyer would enjoy. Armed with an extreme materialism that obliged him to acknowledge only what his five senses could apprehend, and governed only by personal whim and self-interest, Bazarov acted "everywhere and in everything" only as he wished or as seemed to him "profitable and convenient." "Neither over himself, nor outside himself, nor within himself does he acknowledge any regulator, any moral law, any principle." That such freedom might be a basis for anarchy Pisarev plainly foresaw, since he considered it necessary to answer the question as to why Bazarov does not turn to crime. But his answer was unconvincing. Only circumstances and personal taste, he wrote, make such men as Bazarov "honest" or "dishonest," "civic dignitaries" or "inveterate swindlers." Nothing but personal taste, he continued in terms strikingly pertinent to *Crime and Punishment,* "prevents them from killing and robbing" and nothing but personal taste "prompts people of this stamp to make discoveries in the field of science and public life." Pisarev did invoke rational egoism as a restraining factor: intelligent people realize that "it is very profitable to be honest and that any crime, starting with a simple lie and ending with homicide, is dangerous and, consequently, inconvenient." But the die was cast. Pisarev, as Masaryk has put it, had "vindicated for the nihilists the right to kill and to rob."

Those who are capable of exercising the new moral freedom possess great power, as Turgenev, Pisarev and Dostoevsky all realized. They enjoy an implicit superiority over those who remain bound by conventional restraints. In his essay on Bazarov, Pisarev underlined this division of humanity. On the one hand he saw the mass, whose members never use their brains independently. The mass "neither makes discoveries, nor commits crimes"; it lives quietly from day to day "according to the established norm." On the other hand he saw the intelligent individuals who cannot come to terms so easily with all that the mass accepts. These individuals fall into three categories. Firstly, there are those who, being uneducated, are unable properly to take themselves in hand when they withdraw from the herd. Secondly, there are those who are educated but incapable of carrying their rebellion beyond a theoretical stage. And thirdly, there are those who are capable of implementing in practice their theoretical rebellion. These "people of the third category" (*tret'yego razryada*) "acknowledge their dissimilarity to the mass and boldly mark themselves off from it by their acts, by their habits, by their whole way of life. . . . Here the individual attains his full self-liberation, his full individuality and independence." Chernyshevsky, at the end of his publicistic career, draws a somewhat similar distinction in *What Is to Be Done?* between "ordinary people" and those who are by implication extraordinary, although now the rational egoists Lopukhov and Kirsanov (who, as their names imply, have grown symbolically out of Turgenev's representatives of the young generation) are themselves only ordinary before the epitome of independence, the iron-willed "special man" Rakhmetov.

Now Raskolnikov's speculative article on crime which is discussed in part 3 of *Crime and Punishment* owes much to current views such as Pisarev's on the division of mankind into the enslaved and the liberated. Indeed Raskolnikov says that what he is describing "has been printed and read a thousand times" (part 3, chap. 5). Like Pisarev, as Dostoevsky saw him, Raskolnikov has not merely flirted with rational egoism but has "gone further." He aspires, like Bazarov, to membership of that category of people who are bound by no moral law and who may waive those moral considerations that have generally restrained men from committing antisocial acts and continue to prevent the masses from doing so. Thus Raskolnikov has granted himself licence to destroy human life. He has committed the murder and robbery which Pisarev's destroyers might contemplate and has pondered the scientific discoveries and contributions to society which they might make if "personal taste" disposed them to such actions. And he has murdered, it now appears, for no sound financial reason, but merely to confirm the freedom Pisarev had exalted. He is one of those who might be able to say a "*new word*," the original contribution which Pisarev urged his readers not to stifle. His terms of reference are those of Pisarev too, although he has carried out a further simplification: the first category (*pervyy razryad*) is the mass, conservative by nature, which lies obediently; the second category (*vtoroy razryad*) consists of the "extraordinary" men and women, the "people of the future," the "destroyers" (*razrushiteli*) (part 3, chap. 5). Finally, the elitism implicit in Pisarev's schema is reflected in Raskolnikov's pride, his arrogance towards "ordinary" mortals. It is a trait which Dostoevsky is concerned to underline at this particular point in the novel. Thus in the notes for part 3 he remarks that the "thought of immeasurable pride, arrogance, and contempt for society" are expressed in Raskolnikov's personality; and in the finished work Razumikhin tells Raskolnikov's mother and sister that his friend is "arrogant and proud" (part 3, chap. 2).

Raskolnikov, then, represents Dostoevsky's conception of the man moulded by the new outlook and once all inhibitions have been properly stripped away. The self-will of this man accounts for a number of other traits in Raskolnikov's character which are brought out in the novel together with the explanation of the murder of Alyona as an attempt to test Raskolnikov's right to destroy, namely: the violence which threatens to erupt again at the expense of Luzhin; Raskolnikov's inflexible insistence on having his own way, manifested in his determination, of which his mother now speaks, to marry his landlady's crippled daughter (part 3, chap. 2) and his demand that Dunya reject Luzhin (part 3, chap. 3); and his own rejection of all authority, parental and divine, implied by his coolness towards and alienation from his mother and by spurning of prayer once he feels secure (part 2, chap. 7). But most importantly, self-will finds expression in his attitude towards crime which now seems only a further logical consequence of the thorough rejection of all those "constraints," "prejudices" and "traditions" execrated by Pisarev.

VI

As Dostoevsky deepens the examination of the implications of current radical theory, so he broadens his consideration of crime, or more correctly, as the Russian word *prestupleniye* implies, of transgression. He now broaches important questions concerning the general rules by which the conduct of all individuals in a society is circumscribed, namely the laws. There thus begins in his work that profound debate on the nature and status of law which culminates in his last novel and crowning achievement, *The Brothers Karamazov*.

The word "law," of course, may have not only a juridical sense of a "body of enacted or customary rules recognized by a community as binding," but also, among many others, a moral sense of "precepts" or "binding injunctions" to be followed because they are dictated by conscience rather than by statute; and, thirdly, a scientific sense of "correct statement of invariable sequence between specified conditions and specified phenomenon." The variety of meanings inherent in the English word "law" is also available in its Russian equivalent *zakon,* although in Soviet lexicography the moral sense tends to be either blurred, merging with the morally neutral concept of a "generally accepted rule," or simply classified as obsolete.

Numerous Western jurists have discussed the relationship of law in its juridical sense (which may be known as "human," "positive" or "temporal" law) to law in some broader and more abstract sense. They have considered whether there exists a "natural law," that is a "system of right or justice held to be common to all mankind," and have asked themselves whether human law is an expression of such "natural law." Does human law then embody some principles of absolute, universal and permanent validity, can it be evaluated against certain immutable standards? Or does it merely reflect the values and needs of a particular society, and therefore have little or no relevance in other times and places? (The debate is analogous to that on the question as to whether moral values are absolute or relative.) Now Dostoevsky, as a Russian Orthodox writer passionately critical of most tendencies in Western thought, cannot be closely identified with any Western exponents or opponents of theories of natural law, but he is preoccupied with the sort of questions to which Western jurists have addressed themselves, and on one level *Crime and Punishment* represents his first major attempt to deal with them.

Law in its juridical sense—and it is with the "juridical question" that Raskolnikov's remarks to Porfiry in part 3 begin; indeed Raskolnikov has been a student of this law—has little status for Dostoevsky's antihero in his murderous frame of mind. It is clear that the concept lacks absolute authority for him, since he treats it in the same relativistic fashion as crime in part 1 and again in part 3. All the great "lawgivers" to whom he refers—the Spartan Lycurgus, the Athenian Solon, Mohammed and Napoleon (remembered in Russia not only as an invader but also as the promulgator of a new legal code on which Speransky largely based the code he was preparing for Alexander I)—were at the same time "criminals" by virtue of the fact that they destroyed orders sanctified by their forebears. Conversely, just as an act which might normally be deemed a crime was "not a crime" when seen from Raskolnikov's utilitarian point of view in part 1, so the infringement of a law by a Lycurgus might with a similar change of perspective be seen as the establishment of a law. Lawbreakers or "destroyers" might also be designated "lawgivers" and "institutors" (*ustanoviteli*) of mankind (part 3, chap. 5).

Historically speaking, the view that human law had some absolute validity, derived from the existence of an immutable moral law which it expressed, was weakened by the promotion of law in its third, scientific, sense. For thinkers like Comte, who accepted only those concepts which could be verified empirically, rejected as obsolete unproven hypotheses about the existence of God or the nature of man on which moral law rested. They were interested not so much in assumptions about how man ought to behave as in the description and classification of the ways in which he in fact did behave. Again Darwin, in demonstrating scientifically the adaptability of organisms in the struggle for survival, provided a biological precedent for thinkers who urged institutional and legal change in response to external pressures. In this respect, therefore, he too helped to undermine the view that legal orders rest on some permanently valid principle.

The Russian radical thinkers of the 1860s, much influenced by Comte, Darwin and other Western writers who adopted a supposedly scientific approach to the problems that interested them, also treated as absolute and binding only the empirically verifiable scientific law and rejected any intuited natural *laws*. They insisted that a rational man could acknowledge only the empirical method of enquiry which proceeded along the lines of Comte's "positive philosophy" and treated "all phenomena as subject to immutable natural law." Such laws as had already been discovered in the natural sciences they propagated with enthusiasm and every effort was made to reveal equally immutable laws in disciplines such as the study of man's behaviour and even his aesthetic concepts, which had not previously been considered amenable to scientific treatment. Thus Chernyshevsky assured his readers that "all the diversity" in human motivation and in human life in general sprang "from one and the same nature in accordance with one and the same law" and set out to investigate the "laws in accordance with which the heart and the will operate." Pisarev's thought is coloured by the same admiration of the natural sciences and the same faith in the universal applicability of the scientific method.

It is clear from the way in which Raskolnikov frequently expresses his thoughts in *Crime and Punishment* that he too, like many other members of his generation, is a devotee of the scientific method. Just as the student has done in part 1, he presents in part 3 a mathematical equation, in which the discoveries of Kepler and Newton are weighed against the lives of "one, ten, a hundred and so forth people who might prevent this discovery or might stand in the way as an obstacle" (part 3, chap. 5). He neatly divides humanity into "two categories" and repeats the terms "first category" and "second category" and expresses qualifications parenthetically as if in a mathematical formula. And towards the end of his monologue he uses an image already popular with Dostoevsky to evoke the scientific approach (part 2, chap. 4), alluding to the "retort" in which the processes he has described are taking place. He also says now that there must exist some "law of nature" which determines the "order of appearance of people, of all these categories and subdivisions." He is convinced that an exact law governs the divisions of men into the categories he has postulated: "there certainly is and must be a definite law." Nor does the fact that such a law has not yet been discovered shake Raskolnikov's conviction that "it exists and may subsequently become known" (part 3, chap. 5).

In appealing to scientific law Raskolnikov is in effect arguing not only that people who have a new word to say will inevitably break the established criminal law, but also that such people will inevitably appear. This scientific explanation of lawbreaking in turn diminishes the status of any moral law from which human law might have derived from authority. For the scientific inevitability of lawbreaking tends to reduce the culpability of the lawbreakers. A moral choice is valuable if there is freedom to make it. But if actions, in Büchner's words, are in the final analysis "dependent upon a fixed necessity" and if therefore "in every individual case free choice has only an extremely limited, if any, sphere of action," then criminals "are rather deserving of pity than of disgust." And the smaller the degree of control a man has over his actions, the smaller becomes the burden of guilt he must bear for them. The legal implications of this argument were clear to the positivist criminologists of the second half of the nineteenth century, who "instead of assuming a moral stance that focussed on measuring the criminal's 'guilt' and 'responsibility,' . . . attempted a morally neutral and social interpretation of crime and its treatment." If crime was the result of abnormalities in the human organism or of inherited or environmental factors outside the control of the criminal, punishment was an inappropriate response to it. Raskolnikov himself, in invoking scientific law to confirm his right to kill, is brushing aside moral law and thereby detracting from his guilt: he seems, as the horrified Razumikhin notices, to permit the shedding of blood in accordance with the dictates of one's conscience, and he does not expect the "extraordinary" man to suffer if he kills; indeed the greater the calculable utility of his act, the less significant will be the burden of moral responsibility he will bear (part 3, chap. 5).

The ascendancy of a scientific law, then, allows certain people to break the moral law as well as human law with impunity. Thus as law in one of its senses is promoted, so the status of law in another of its senses is diminished. The "men of the sixties," who had shown such industry in redefining concepts and values such as the "beautiful" and the "good," had also shifted the emphasis of the concept of law from the morally binding to the scientifically inevitable. Indeed in so far as the "extraordinary" men are granted free will, it had become morally binding, Dostoevsky implies, for them to promote what was scientifically indisputable. For the establishment of scientific laws seems in part 3 of *Crime and Punishment* to have become the most pressing moral obligation. Kepler and Newton, to whom Raskolnikov refers in support of his thesis that "extraordinary people" may "step over" certain "obstacles," are unaggressive scientists whose association in Raskolnikov's mind with Napoleon seems at first sight strange. In fact they constitute classic examples of the discoverers of physical laws of motion of the sort admired for their apparent incontestability by the men of the sixties. (Thus in *What Is to Be Done?* Newton is extolled by Rakhmetov as the "most brilliant and the most sane mind of all the minds known to us.") And to Raskolnikov the promotion of the discoveries of these scientists had evidently seemed so important that what might normally have been designated a "crime" could have been in a sense quite legitimately committed in order to assist it. Raskolnikov seems to imply by his choice of examples, then, that the cause of the transgression of the law may be the need to establish a scientific law and even that such a transgression is obligatory. For although in one breath he denies that he insists, as he thinks Porfiry has insinuated, that "extraordinary people inevitably must and always were bound to commit all sorts of excesses," he does in the next admit that a Newton, encountering obstacles to the dissemination of his discoveries, "would have the right, and would even be obliged" to eliminate the individuals standing in his way (part 3, chap. 5).

VII

It is a repeatedly asserted or implied belief of Dostoevsky's in the early 1860s that his radical contemporaries were wrong to concede omnicompetence to law in its scientific sense. By devising and upholding such law they neither provided an entirely accurate description of man's nature and conduct nor did they lay down sound rules about how he ought to behave.

Just as the observation of a utilitarian ethic tended to reduce to impersonal mathematical terms problems of human conduct which were properly speaking unquantifiable, so the attempt to bring all man's characteristics and behaviour under the jurisdiction of scientific laws resulted in an oversimplification of a very complex reality. In attempting to embrace reality in its entirety in some logically incontestable schema, the radicals failed properly to take into account aspects of man's being other than his reason; for phenomena which were not rational, or the existence of which could not be empirically demonstrated, did not seem to lend themselves to precise analysis. The exponents of the supposedly scientific doctrines, Dostoevsky wrote in his notebook, were "theoreticians" who wished to "clip" man, to shear off him those parts of his being which did not accord with the soothing theories they had devised in the isolation of their studies or which might serve to obstruct the development of the utopias they envisaged. There are references to such simplification in *Crime and Punishment* too: Razumikhin, for example, accuses the socialists of failing to take human nature into account when designing their phalansteries. "All the mysteries of life" they try to accommodate "on two printer's sheets" (part 3, chap. 5). In particular the radicals seemed to Dostoevsky to ignore man's often irrational craving to assert his individuality, to preserve at least that illusion of free will so cherished by the Underground Man. They also failed to take into consideration conscience, the "moral sense of right and wrong" which might inhibit harsh treatment of one's fellows. Individual conscience, having no bearing on the general utility of an action, is not a faculty to which the student in part 1 of *Crime and Punishment* is prepared to devote serious attention. And Raskolnikov, treating it more as an attribute of the oppressed mass than as an innate human characteristic, expects to remain free of the remorse it might arouse.

In opposition to the supposedly irrefutable scientific laws exalted by the radicals, Dostoevsky puts forward certain laws of his own which seem to him more accurately to describe reality as he perceives it. There is a "law of truth and human nature," he writes in his letter to Katkov, which leads the criminal voluntarily to accept "torments." The suffering required by the criminal and described by Porfiry as a "great thing" (part 6, chap. 2) contrasts with the pleasure which utilitarianism postulates as the only end of man's existence. It is a law of nature for Porfiry, moreover, that a criminal like Raskolnikov, pursued by psychological methods, and left at large in the uncertainty dreaded by the rationalist, will eventually trap himself (part 4, chap. 5). And "facts"—the investigator's equivalent of scientific data, which it is not really proper for him to question (part 6, chap. 2)—Porfiry treats with scepticism, for they may lead him into error no less than the "abstract arguments of reason" which have so beguiled Raskolnikov (part 4, chap. 5).

Not only does Dostoevsky suggest the existence of psychological laws at variance with those accepted by the radicals (whose approach to psychology, as Dostoevsky perceives it, is reflected in *Crime and Punishment* in the statements of Zosimov on the subject (e.g., part 3, chap. 1). More importantly Dostoevsky also reinstates the moral law which scientific law tended to ignore or to suppress. The moral law emanated not from the reason—only a "twentieth part" of the Underground Man's capacity for living—but from the spiritual side of man's nature which, Chernyshevsky had categorically stated, did not exist. In opposition to Chernyshevsky's supposedly scientific law, which asserted that egoism was the basic impulse of all human actions, Dostoevsky's moral law postulated in man a need for "sacrifice," the submission of one's ego to others in selfless love. It is clearly this law which Dostoevsky believes will prevail in the final stage of human development, designated "Christianity" and envisaged by him in plans for an article drafted shortly before he embarked on the writing of *Crime and Punishment*. The Christian phase would supplant and stand in opposition to a phase designated "civilization," characterized by the extreme development of the individual consciousness and crowned by the advent of socialism. And it is Christ's commandment "Thou shalt love thy neighbour as thyself," observed in *Crime and Punishment* by Sonya, which ultimately prohibits acts based on the supposedly scientific precept approved by Luzhin, "Love, above all, thyself alone" (part 2, chap. 5).

For Dostoevsky the moral law, not any scientific law, is sovereign: there is "one law—the moral law," he wrote in a rough draft of one of the scenes of the novel. Beside this law human law pales into insignificance. Thus Porfiry, although he is the chief agent of the human law in *Crime and Punishment,* is manifestly "less concerned with apprehending Raskolnikov as a criminal," as Richard Peace has aptly put it, "than with saving him as a human being." In any case the "[juridical] punishment for a crime," Dostoevsky wrote in his letter to Katkov, "frightens a criminal much less than they [the lawgivers] think, in part because *he himself morally requires* it." But the unimportance of the human law beside the moral law does not entitle one to break it. For whereas the promotion of supposedly scientific laws tended to weaken existing legal codes by making crime a relative concept, the reinstatement of moral law strengthened them by making acts such as killing absolutely wrong. Raskolnikov therefore does not have the right to disregard human law on the grounds that its authority is threatened by inevitable political, social or intellectual change; on the contrary, he is bound to obey it because it expresses a higher Christian principle.

VIII

The points I have made stand in need of three qualifications. Firstly, Dostoevsky was not a singleminded publicist, like Chernyshevsky, but first and foremost an artist committed to faithful and full representation of reality as he perceived it; he did not therefore give definitive answers to the questions he posed. Secondly, some of the views implicit in *Crime and Punishment* were not fully developed by Dostoevsky for more than another decade, until he presented that profound debate which takes place in *The Brothers Karamazov* on the relationship between the "laws of Christ" and the laws of the state and on the need to punish the criminal by cutting off not a limb but a soul. And thirdly, to read the novel primarily as a contribution to the intellectual life of the period is to illuminate it only partially and to leave out of consideration its artistic riches and other qualities.

Nevertheless it is true to say that Dostoevsky, unlike Turgenev, did have passionate convictions which find expression in his novels. Moreover, Dostoevsky's objections to the new radical *Weltanschauung* had on the whole become clear by the time he came to write *Crime and Punishment* in 1865. Most importantly, it was probably mainly out of a desire to state or at least to clarify these objections that Dostoevsky now raised numerous important questions. Is man's behaviour determined by circumstances outside his control? Is he bound, if placed in certain conditions, to commit crime? Should criminals be considered blameless for their actions? Is it unjust that criminals should suffer punishment? Is the individual unimportant by comparison with the larger group to which he belongs? Do affirmative answers to these questions help to promote crime by destroying in the individual a sense of responsibility for his actions and love and respect for his fellows? And it is in no small measure from Dostoevsky's examination of these questions—to which radical contemporaries seemed to give such crude and dogmatic answers—that *Crime and Punishment* derives its lasting and universal significance.

Crime and Punishment: Theory and Life

John Jones

In the mid-1860s Dostoevsky developed a marked tendency to fuss about the relation between real life and fiction, between the goings-on in the newspapers and what he was saying or wanted to say in his novels. I stress the newspapers. He was altogether more interested, on the surface at any rate, in what he found there than in what he could observe of people and events around him. A draft letter to his publisher Katkov—the fair copy is lost—discusses the plot of the as yet unwritten *Crime and Punishment*. It states defensively:

> You'll find in our newspapers many signs of an extraordinary mental instability leading to terrible deeds (that theological student who killed a girl he had arranged to meet in a shed, and who was arrested an hour later eating his breakfast—and so on). In short, I'm convinced my theme is partly justified by contemporary life.

For once he was underplaying his hand. *Crime and Punishment* did not merely reflect or even confirm that strange and removed elsewhere, the world journalists write about. It anticipated that world. Readers were settling down to the novel's opening instalment—not a venture to be recommended for "people with weak nerves" remarked Strakhov, the gifted critic—when a murder story broke in the newspapers. Danilov, a student who had tried to live by private teaching, intelligent, handsome, dark-haired, solitary, killed and robbed a money-lender and his maid. In the course of the trial one Glazkov made a false confession which he later re-

From *Dostoevsky*. © 1983 by John Jones. Oxford University Press, 1983.

tracted. The newspapers themselves leaped on the parallel with Raskolnikov and his crime and with the innocent Nikolai's declaration of guilt. Nature had followed art. Danilov, *The Voice* observed, had probably not
even begun to contemplate his murder when Dostoevsky was shaping
Raskolnikov's. The two cases were laid side by side, and likenesses and
differences were solemnly analysed as if we had here before us two "real,"
directly comparable objects. All this brought joy to the novelist. He often
spoke to Strakhov of his "pride as an author" in his creative foreshadow-
ing of facts, and to A. N. Maikov he enlarged:

> Oh my friend, I have completely different notions of reality
> and realism from our realists and critics. My idealism is much
> more real than theirs [meaning "than their realism"]. . . . Their
> realism won't help you explain a hundredth part of the real
> events which have actually occurred. But we by our idealism
> have even prophesied events. It has happened.

We are on familiar ground, since this idealism is none other than his
deeper—sometimes he called it deepest, sometimes highest—realism; but
with new implications in that he is beginning to show a sensitiveness to
the actual which no doubt existed before but was rarely evident, a sensitiveness which is now coming out like a bruise. This is an important aspect of the process I have called his working his way backwards into the
nineteenth century. *Crime and Punishment* takes its place in a perfectly obvious and open fashion among the international classics of naturalism (or realism), and it is the first of his novels to do so: the earlier and great book
The House of the Dead walks so close beside personal history as to rule itself
out in this connection; formally it is a freak, so I argued, a quasi-novel;
and as regards fact and fiction, since he is recounting not "prophesying
events," Dostoevsky cannot have found much in the Dead House to get
excited about.

Whereas in *Crime and Punishment* and in the novels which follow he
can, though his narrow glee over being ahead of the fact is unworthy of
his art and of what "idealism" and "deeper realism" intend. Shrewd guess-
ing at tendency is not the jewel in his casket. The interest of how things
are resides in their figuration, discernible and expressible by the deeper realist, of how things will be only in so far as that futurity is the truth and
the end of how they are and always have been. His naturalism is apocalyptic. The social and psychological trends that were bound to produce
Raskolnikov/Danilov are the mere phenomenology of a transcendent mystic and biblical cryptogram. The Book of Revelation, which Tolstoy said

"reveals absolutely nothing," is more heavily marked than anything else in the New Testament which Dostoevsky took to prison with him, and we know that huge overarching shapes like Baal, the Kingdom of Antichrist, are beginning to appear in his writing from the early 1860s. Danilov's double murder looks small beer in comparison. Indeed it is pertinent to ask what scope of revelatory prophecy *Crime and Punishment* is aiming at.

An ambitious impression is created by Raskolnikov's delirium and nightmare:

> In his illness he dreamt that the whole world was condemned to fall victim to some terrible and unknown pestilence that was coming upon Europe out of the depths of Asia. All were doomed to perish except a chosen few, a very few. There appeared a new strain of trichinae, microscopic creatures parasitic upon the bodies of human beings. But these creatures were spirits endowed with intelligence and will. People who were infected by them immediately became as men possessed and out of their minds.

A grand and dread apocalypse. But this occurs in *Crime and Punishment*'s epilogue. It is aftermath rather than the novel itself. And the epilogue also points forward in its closing words to "a new tale," because "our present one is ended," and the narrator says he has in mind the slow regeneration of Raskolnikov, now in prison, through love and suffering. No such novel ever got written. But Raskolnikov's nightmare calls to mind one that did, namely *The Possessed,* while the specific link between "as men possessed" (*besnovatimi*) and *The Possessed* (*Besi,* literally *The Devils*) is inescapably obvious—just as the word "Socialism" which Dostoevsky has written against the beast in Revelation coming out of the earth with horns like a lamb and speech like a dragon shows the general way his thoughts are tending.

And again this is the way of *The Possessed* rather than *Crime and Punishment.* However, a second marginal comment in his New Testament both latches on to *Crime and Punishment* and provokes a backward thought. His note on the beast of chapter 17 of Revelation, the beast which doesn't exist and still has to appear and is destined for perdition, is "generalhuman"—the word he coined for *Notes from Underground* and incidentally never used again in his fiction. At the end of the Underground Man's tirade "generalhumans" appears as the notional creatures we are trying to turn ourselves into because "we feel it's too much of a burden to be men—men with real bodies, real blood *of our own.*" How can we have any other bodies and blood than our own? We can't. We can only think about it. And *Notes from Underground* is precisely such a fable of disembodied consciousness.

But in the opening paragraphs of *Crime and Punishment* consciousness has found a home in the unnamed and very physical young man who leaves his stuffy little top room and slips downstairs like a cat, out into the street. This young man is also very mental. His being is riddled with theory and hypothesis. He has a plan. Rather, he has a plan of a plan: the plan being to murder an old money-lender, while the plan of that plan is to embark here and now, out of doors, in the glare and summer stench of Petersburg, upon a rehearsal of the murder.

The question of motive hangs over these first pages, and over the whole novel. Dostoevsky's letter to Katkov asserting that crimes like Raskolnikov's can be found in the newspapers also discusses motive. The old money-lender with her "Jewish" interest rates is to be murdered because her life is worthless and her hoarded wealth can be put to good use; when the unimportant deed is done the doer will launch himself into something that really matters, a large-scale philanthropic exercise. But *Crime and Punishment* didn't work out like that. The letter to Katkov belongs to the autumn of 1865. Between then and the end of the year Dostoevsky put aside every word he had written and began again. And in this new version the philanthropic rationalist and utilitarian Raskolnikov has almost completely disappeared. And in his place we have a murderer fascinated by the Napoleonic idea.

Repeatedly, he says that to brush a vicious old woman aside like a swatted fly and get on with life is to prove oneself a Napoleon—not Napoleon himself who lost whole armies and forgot about them, but *a* Napoleon. He finds out that there is no such person. In *a* Napoleon he cannot discover anybody to be; *a* Napoleon is a projected, dreamed-up, aimed-at type, a "generalhuman." Dostoevsky's homemade word doesn't appear in *Crime and Punishment*; it has been left behind (unlike the mind that coined it) in the much more theoretical *Notes from Underground*. With Raskolnikov the issue has been naturalized into a restless and greedy discontent. "Mere existence had never been enough for him; he had always wanted something more."

And it follows from this calculatedly vague "something more" that the Napoleonic idea doesn't settle the question of motive either. Its domination of the final text only means that it is Raskolnikov's favourite way of rationalizing his malaise. Nothing in him matches his deed. Dostoevsky exhorted himself in his notebooks to "explain the whole murder *one way or another* and make its character and relations clear, but the artist in him wouldn't allow it. On one occasion, lashing about for reasons after the event, Raskolnikov cries out "I simply wanted to dare, Sonya, that was my only motive"; and next to "I just did it" this must be reckoned his least untrue account of himself and his deed. Wanting to dare is his opposite number to the underground man's wanting to want, because whereas wanting to want holds fast to the earlier novel's metaphysical spareness and abstraction, wanting to dare opens up the whole huge circumstance of the murder itself, the thing that in fact gets done.

II

Though Conrad's *Narcissus* runs it close, *Crime and Punishment* remains for me the most accessible and exciting novel in the world. It is the king of murder stories. And of detective stories. And of thrillers. Its atmosphere and suspense are nursed by locality—Petersburg—in ways which can't be escaped but which often get misreported. Commentators are fond of discovering and praising a guidebook clarity in the novel. They have been deceived by the plethora of street names, bridges, islands, and so forth. All these topographical details are there and are correct. But they don't cohere, don't add up. You couldn't find your way round this city any more (and here is a strange thought) than you have got the practical hang of the little fortress prison at Omsk by the end of *The House of the Dead*. To compare Raskolnikov's haymarket with Kim's bazaar is to see that Kipling has done all the work so that you don't have to go there to know what it's like at the level of vivid and varied description, whereas Dostoevsky leaves his reader with an impression which hovers between smell and vapour and dream.

In fact the street names and the rest belong with the extremely important disjunctive flotsam of the book: paint-pots, old rope, the odd sock, boots that once belonged to the Secretary at the English Embassy, twists of paper, egg-shells, fish-guts, frayed blood-soaked strips torn from trouser-bottoms and coat-pockets, an axe-sling in ribbons ("Little bits of torn linen cannot possibly arouse suspicion!"), half-eaten meals, small change, miscellaneous pawned objects, candle-ends, trousseau-stuff ("fancy boxes, dressing-cases, ornaments, dress material, and all that sort of junk from Knopf's and the English Shop"), broken crocks (*cherepki*), and skulls (*cherepi*). And what the commentators are really paying homage to, what prompts their sense of coherence and a world revealed, is a feat of illusionist sorcery. In a notebook, beneath the underlined word "tone" and "NB" penned three times, Dostoevsky has written among other jottings "summer, dust, mortar"; and in this case the man and the artist are at one. *This is the city* which readers of *Crime and Punishment* carry with them for the rest of their lives. The novelist stayed away from "stinking Petersburg" during the unbearably hot summer of 1866, to avoid his creditors but also on his guard against what he called "false inspiration." He relied on his mind's eye and ear—and nose. The result is a townscape of "terrible despairing cries" which mean, and mean more than, that the drunks are leaving the pubs between two and three o'clock in the morning, the pubs that reek of alcohol and cucumber and fish. A townscape of nightmare yellows: sky, buildings, furniture, wallpaper, faces—the colour of age, heat, pestilence, bile and jaundice, bruisings and stainings, with a stronger connotation of dirt in Russian than in English; the colour of the tickets of identification which prostitutes were required to carry; the colour of Raskolnikov's "cubby-hole" of a room; and the colour which greets him when he comes to after fainting at the police station and sees a man "holding a yellow glass filled with yellow water."

Looking over Dostoevsky's shoulder, we find him first writing "small yellow glass," then deleting "small"; and writing "water," then adding "yellow warm" to the water, then deleting "warm"—the final text uniting an apocalyptic starkness of yellow meets yellow with the topicality of Petersburg's notoriously filthy water supply, a subject of much comment and complaint in the newspapers. At such moments we come as close as it is possible to get to the spirit of *Crime and Punishment*. Having, as I say, abandoned everything he had done, he sat down and wrote a six-part novel within a year which included a twenty-six day break in which he threw together and dictated *The Gambler,* itself not a small book nor a negligible one, to satisfy the terms of a contract he had made with a shyster publisher. "The very thought would be enough to kill Turgenev," so he told a friend, and posterity salutes a marvel of concentrated effort. He wrote month after month with fearful haste, and yet the Soviet editor only exaggerates slightly when he says that the manuscripts reveal "immense, most rigorous work, literally over every phrase." This combination of speed and close attention may have a lot to do with the narrative thrust and atmospheric coherence and intensity that make this the most gripping of his novels.

Then there's the energy generated by frustration. The thing had refused to come right. His notebooks show him hesitating between reminiscence ("It was exactly eight years ago") and testimony during trial ("I am on trial and will tell everything"). Note the "I." He was thinking in terms of first-person narrative—Raskolnikov's own story. This proved unmanageable. Much of what the novelist wanted to say lay outside the murderer's ken, and, as we shall see, Raskolnikov's consciousness was in other, subtler ways too confining.

Also, Raskolnikov's narrative was to have been "A Confession"—Dostoevsky's own title—and this wouldn't work either. We recall that the confessional idea has a long history. First the pre-Siberian "confessions." Next the unrealized plan for a full-length novel, *Confession,* which got switched to the short *Notes from Underground.* And now another failure. And still, after *Crime and Punishment,* the idea of a confession novel or story tugs at the edge of Dostoevsky's vision, and continues to do so for the rest of his life in the form of *The Life of a Great Sinner* which he planned on the scale of *War and Peace,* but which never got written though it fed previous material into his novels of the seventies, and especially *Karamazov* at the turn of the next decade. (Dmitry didn't kill his father but he keeps baring his breast to people about how much he wanted to.)

So the idea of Raskolnikov's "Confession" ran into the ground. But there it encountered another ruined project, a work to be called *The Drunks* of which only a tiny fragment survives, and the marriage of these two constitutes the success of *Crime and Punishment.* The drink theme too, broadly understood, goes back a very long way. Behind the truant husband Marmeladov, perhaps the greatest feat of instant creation in all Dostoevsky as he buttonholes Raskolnikov in the pub with hay sticking to his clothes and vodka at hand—behind that immortal Russian drunkard stretches a long line of urban dropouts and psychological cripples, of paupers and other victims of the ravages of early capitalism (think of Petersburg as several decades behind Manchester), of the "insulted and injured" in the novel of that title and elsewhere, back to the beginning, back to Mr Devushkin with his teapot and pipe and his "fearful lapses" over the bottle.

Why does Marmeladov drink? The *Crime and Punishment* notebooks expend considerable effort trying to establish an overarching reason or at least an empirical scatter of factors, and failing. Compare Dostoevsky's attempt, frustrated by the good angel of his genius, to explain Raskolnikov's motive for his crime. In the novel itself, where we might expect Marmeladov to speak of solace, respite, forgetting, companionship, he grasps the parodox that he drinks because he is in search of suffering, of "tears and tribulation." And, he adds, "I have found them." This has the same free, metaphysical bearing on his being a drunkard that Raskolnikov's wanting to dare has on his being a murderer. Moreover, as always in Dostoevsky, the search for suffering refuses to settle into coherent masochistic focus.

Marmeladov's wife, he says, "has a consumptive tendency, and I feel it. How could I not feel it? And the more I drink the more I feel it. Indeed that's why I drink, to find compassion and feeling in drink. It's not happiness but sorrow that I'm looking for. I drink because I want to suffer more and more." So his intensified sorrow is the intensified compassion and feeling for his wife which drink whips up. This is the Marmeladov who married his present wife—not that that did any good either—because he could not bear to see such suffering. We have here the grand selfish selfless nonlogic, the deeper realism, of his drinking.

And so the drunkard wants to suffer, while the murderer wants to dare. The one is the passive and the other the active form of a single human truth, as Dostoevsky sees it and realizes it fictionally. The singleness of this truth is what I called the marriage of the *Drunks* project and the "Confession" project in *Crime and Punishment*. The novelist is now of course in middle age, but right back in his teens he wrote to his brother "Man is a mystery," adding that a lifetime spent trying to unravel the mystery would not be wasted. On its own this reads like a perfectly ordinary youthful Europeanized sententious romantic flourish. But now comes the idiosyncratic twist. "I am devoting myself to this mystery because I want to be a man." He doesn't mean that he wants to become mature or to quell the beast within or anything else comfortable to the understanding. It's a very personal way of thinking and writing which we have encountered several times already, and which now, twenty-seven years after that letter to his brother, appears most insistently with Raskolnikov as he "paused for a moment to take breath, to collect himself, and to enter *as a man*" and tell the police who it was killed the old money-lender and her sister. But since *Crime and Punishment* encompasses the drinking as well as the confessional theme, we can approach Dostoevsky's abiding human question—what is it to be a man?—also by way of the minuscule *Drunks* fragment:

> "The reason we drink is we're at a loose end."
> "Nonsense. We drink because we've got no morals."
> "Yes, and the reason we've got no morals is that for a long
> time (150 years) we've been at a loose end."

And that's all. Put most simply, being at a loose end leads men to the vice of drunkenness and the crime of murder; and the jobless Marmeladov and the ex-student Raskolnikov are both very pointedly at a loose end. But to say that the devil finds work for idle hands to do is misleading because hypermoralistic or (if meant literally) hypertheological. In that little exchange which is the entire *Drunks* fragment the "loose end" idea under-cuts the moral and every other aspect of the matter, and once again there's a link with journalism, this time Dostoevsky's own. He specifies 150 years because he has in mind the social and political reforms of Peter the Great in the early eighteenth century. This subject had interested him, both as contributor to and editor of the magazines *Time* and *Epoch* in the years immediately before he wrote *Crime and Punishment.* He believed that Pe-ter's reforms had disrupted society by creating a Western-type bourgeoisie and separating the educated class from the common people. What Peter had damaged, and what one might hope to restore, was the natural soil-based unity of Russia. And so, as in *Winter Notes,* Dostoevsky is really talking about *pochvennost,* his own brand of romantic conservatism, half history, half dream.

In *Crime and Punishment* itself the Petrine reforms get the merest glanc-ing reference, and only one, when Raskolnikov's friend Razumikhin speaks of "us" (compare the "we" of the *Drunks* fragment) as "divorced from practical affairs of every sort for nearly two hundred years." This is a hasty throw-off in the middle of a wide-ranging argument, and it has no particular bearing on drink. Nor for that matter on crime. Nor has it any more to do with Peter's reforms than might perhaps justify an editorial footnote.

But the underlying idea of being at a loose end, or out of the practical swim, is a different matter altogether. It is the very clay out of which Dos-toevsky shapes his fictions of solitude and society. And while it might be said that his version of *pochvennost* comes from this same source, and while it is certainly true that *pochvennost* deserves a longer footnote than the Pe-trine reforms, a footnote is all it should be. For the novelist works to one side—hence parajournalist—of the writer busy with magazine polemics in *Time* and *Epoch,* just as his novel exists to one side—parajournalism—of the double murder in the newspapers and of scary science-fictionish fore-warnings about microbes.

This to-one-side posture of novelist and novel explains how it is that Raskolnikov and Marmeladov are pointedly at a loose end while *Crime and Punishment* is anything but pointedly sociological. The thrust of their loose end, as of details like the murderer's yellow cubby-hole—coffinlike, his mother calls it—and Marmeladov's greenish-yellow face and the mortal yellow-black bruise over the heart after he gets run over, is metaphysical and apocalyptic, not documentary. "Every man must have somewhere to go," Marmeladov tells Raskolnikov who has dropped into the pub after his "rehearsal" of the murder. "For there comes a time when he absolutely must go somewhere." Raskolnikov is young, preoccupied and merely puzzled—"young, abstract and therefore cruel," the severe voice of the novel describes him elsewhere—but the reader attends in tragic wonder, for he understands that Marmeladov has indeed nowhere to go, a nowhere which is the finality of his loose end, at once in character, at once personal to the selfish selfless rationale of one man's marriage and his other circumstances, personal to his "destitution" or "extemity" or "*misère*" (*nishcheta,* which he is careful to distinguish from his poverty), and at the same time an objective and transpersonal theme running through all Dostoevsky's work.

From the novelist's journalism and notebooks and letters we glean the almost comically unresonant information that being at a loose end leads men to drunkenness and murder. His novels, though, suggest a mental movement not unlike Virgil's thought to the effect that bees are working animals and don't retire and spend their sunset years playing golf: being at a loose end is not the condition of us spiritual and working animals, it is not being a man among men. Marmeladov doesn't think of a drunkard as a human being but as a brute, a beast, a swine. He lives a swine and he dies a swine. But on the Last Day certainly God will call the drunkards of the world to Him:

> He will summon us also: "Come forth," He will say, "ye also! Come forth ye drunkards, come forth weak ones, come forth children of shame!" And we shall all come forth, and yet not in shame, and we shall stand before Him. And He will say: "Ye are swine! ye are made in the Image of the Beast and bear his mark; yet come ye also!" And the wise ones and the men of learning shall say: "Lord, why dost thou receive these?" And He shall say: "I receive them, O ye wise ones, I receive them, O ye men of learning, inasmuch as not one of these has deemed himself worthy." And He will stretch forth His arms to us, and we shall fall down before Him and weep, and we shall understand all things.

So the swine—swine in God's eyes too—will appear on Judgment Day immortal souls capable of penitence and knowledge. This tirade, carried on vodka-laden breath, is a classic instance of Dostoevsky's apocalyptic naturalism working on two levels at once. Marmeladov projects the Christian Revelation on the church-slavonic plane of his and every Russian's Bible and liturgy, remoter from everyday usage than the English Authorized Version; and he indulges a maundering drunken account of

himself. The second is an untidy surgical exposure, the more convincing
and moving for its incompetence, of the first's withheld human inward-
ness, while the first is a theological drama in which the *must* of "a man
absolutely must go somewhere" gets tortured on the rack of faith. The
one point on which Mr Golyadkin and Double were agreed was that there
is nobody like God, but it follows pat and false that if a man has nowhere
to go God will look after him. In the notebooks of *Crime and Punishment,*
Marmeladov (at this stage called "the civil servant") is made to argue that
"if only a man is *really alive,* then he suffers, and therefore he needs Christ,
and therefore Christ will come." Such explicitness would be a disaster in
the novel, but it underlies the final text of the pub tirade like a geological
substratum, and it reflects the great and growing importance of mystic suffering in Dostoevsky's post-Siberian work.

Even more damaging would be the inclusion of the following thought
about Raskolnikov: "NB. With the crime itself begins his moral development, the possibility of those questions which didn't exist before. In the
last chapter, in prison, he says that without the crime he would not have
found within himself *such* questions, desires, feelings, needs, strivings, and
development." Were he to say any such thing we would be left with a
therapeutic murder. But again Dostoevsky is fumbling after a creative or
regenerative suffering, because it is of the essence of Raskolnikov's questions, desires, feelings, and so forth (which of course do appear in the
novel) that they should be agonized. The fictional morphology of this suffering is more aptly suggested by the novelist and critic Akhsharumov,
writing the very year *Crime and Punishment* appeared in hard covers, who
observes that Raskolnikov's mental torment, which *is* his punishment in
all but its public aspect, beings with his first promptings towards the
crime.

Thus Akhsharumov directs the reader to something that makes him
certain he holds a masterpiece in his hands before he has read half a dozen
pages: a single prenatal life, a foetal stirring and growth, no ordinary robust narrative sense of something afoot. Raskolnikov's first thought on
slinking down the lodging-house stairs is one of surprise at himself that he
should be "simultaneously" in terror of his landlady and planning a murder. The mental suffering and the evil intent won't be separated. Raskolnikov doesn't put it to himself like that. We do. He is just surprised. On the
surface of his mind lies the contrast between a trivial though tormenting
fear and a monstrous scheme; and beneath that contrast appears a positive
contradiction: for a few sentences earlier we have been told "He was not
really afraid of any landlady."

The question, who tells us? recalls the most important of Dostoevsky's many changes in the course of writing *Crime and Punishment,* his switch from first-person narration—the murderer's story—to what is formally third-person but proves so supple, so volatile, that the distinction between the inside and outside of Raskolnikov's head disappears when his creator wants it to. The solution to "He was not really afraid of any landlady" might appear to be that we have here a masked first-person avowal, and that it is simply an indication of Dostoevsky's boldness that it should be surrounded by authorial statements which are firmly outside and (so to say) on top of Raskolnikov in the classical omniscient third-person mode: for example, information about his poverty, irritable frame of mind, withdrawal from society, his "not naturally timorous and abject" disposition. But masked first-person narrative turns out to be deflected stream of consciousness—"He was not really afraid" will only transpose into "I'm not really afraid" flitting through his head as he passes the landlady's open kitchen door—so that the past tense collapses into the present, and we find we have put our finger on something pertinent to the novel's urgency and attack and (to borrow Andrew Forge's ugly but useful key-term for late Monet) its frontality.

That Raskolnikov is not by nature timorous is the author's assurance to his readers, dependable through nineteenth-century novelistic convention. That Raskolnikov is not really afraid is, in its latent truth and force, what he tells himself. The two narrative modes walk side by side in bold yet relaxed society, and support each other in the face of the fact that Raskolnikov is shaking in his shoes. The author knows (even if Akhsharumov has to remind him) that the natural man in his hero has been laid low by the combined psychic onset of crime and punishment. Raskolnikov knows (but leaves us to infer) that his present state of mind renders chatter on the stairs intolerable, which looks like fear of his landlady but "really" isn't. As to state of mind, Raskolnikov lives with his own continuously but inspects it only intermittently, like the rest of us; whereas the author surveys the whole truth the whole time, so that we never find him wondering whether perhaps Raskolnikov is thinking this or perhaps he is thinking that: a fact which isolates *Crime and Punishment* among the mature novels, because elsewhere Dostoevsky loves the unsettled and unsettling narrative posture of "perhaps," particularly with his contracting and dilating collective voice, the "we" swept by rumour and speculation which arrives in *The House of the Dead* and reaches its full flowering in *The Possessed.*

While *Crime and Punishment*'s author (or omniscient narrator) knows the truth, he picks his moment to tell it. He bides his time. Then he moves in, for example to reveal that the young hero–murderer, once the deed was done, had a completely new experience "of infinite loneliness and estrangement"; and that this experience "was most agonising in that it was a sensation rather than knowledge or intellectual understanding, a direct sensation, the most painful sensation he had ever experienced in his life." Raskolnikov could never have said that—which introduces the deeper issues involved in the switch from first-person to a nominal third-person narrative. Raskolnikov lives with his pain, but most of the time he doesn't focus on it. He rubs it absently, accosting strangers in the street, seeking out a friend and within minutes exclaiming that he wants to be by himself, watching children wistfully, accusing wellwishers of persecuting him with their kindness; until at last he explodes on the brink of confession in a terrible universal cry: "Oh, if only I were alone and nobody loved me, and if only I had never loved anyone!"

Of course he doesn't really want to be alone. He is still just rubbing his pain when he says that. What he *really* wants is a business of the inside and outside of his head, in this case of his "alone" juxtaposed with the authorial "loneliness and estrangement": a rich relationship, not a flat contradiction or dead end, a relationship which evokes and nurses a distinction established as far back as *The Double,* between false solitude ("loneliness and estrangement") and true solitude which is the obverse of true society and meaningless without it.

But occasionally, as I say, Raskolnikov contemplates the pain he lives with:

> The conviction that everything, even memory, even the simple power of understanding, was deserting him, began to torture him unbearably. "What if it is beginning already, what if my punishment is already beginning? Look, over there—I thought so!" And indeed the frayed scrappy edges he had cut off from his trousers were lying strewn on the floor, in the middle of the room for everyone to see! "What on earth can be the matter with me?" he cried again like a man utterly lost.

And this in fact, not in theory, is how crime—the bloody evidence on the floor—and punishment—Raskolnikov's agony—intertwine in the novel. A wonderful moment. It sets one hesitating between general admiration and the attempt to give point to frontality or some such term: anything to obtain leverage on a narrative mode which sweeps up event and idea, fictional past and stream-of-consciousness present, into a single impulse of this immediacy and power.

III

For a moment Raskolnikov wonders if his punishment has already begun. Now the reader met a suffering young man on the first page of the novel. And having met him, he at once began studying him and suffering with him: observing him *ab extra* and sharing the inside of his head; hence his sense that he is both witnessing and experiencing the "strange smile" which accompanies Raskolnikov's surprise at his own dread of meeting his landlady. That "strange" which would be a lazy gesture in another novelist is indeed strange to the reader, strange as the feline, supremely *observed* young man himself; and yet he feels the very muscles and skin-surface of Raskolnikov's smile—a prelude to the way in which the book's entire action is simultaneously read about and lived through.

Common sense may deem this a highfalutin account of a quality possessed by every exciting story. Well yes, in so far as it's a question of degree, though if *Crime and Punishment* really is the king of thrillers then there's something unique to remark in it and even to wax a bit pompous about. For in a monarchy, as Beethoven remarked of Handel, one knows to whom one must bend the knee.

But also: well no. Sometimes there's no question of degree. The wrath of Achilles doesn't work like Dostoevsky's novel at all, and not because it's an old tale. The ship *Narcissus* in her fight to the southward doesn't work like this either. The truth is, not all exciting stories are properly thrillers. Being gripped by a narrative is an altogether wider notion than what is presaged by the two-in-one of being outside yet inside Raskolnikov's "strange smile": the rehearsal of the murder, the murder sequence itself, the three long duels with the detective Porfiry, the suffering, the hesitation, the final climb up the police-station stairs. Dostoevsky's own attempt to suggest how he disposes his reader in relation to these events goes as follows: "Narration by the author, a sort of invisible but omniscient being who nevertheless doesn't leave him [meaning "his hero"] for a moment." So, after appearing to settle for third-person narrative, he doubles back on himself and leaves us to make what we can of an omniscient author who is bound hand and foot to a far from omniscient protagonist.

That he succeeds in having it both ways is our experience of reading his novel in its dominant and thriller aspect. His Petersburg counts for an awful lot. The illusionism which conjures a complete and natural (I would prefer apocalyptic–natural) city out of materials as unpromising as the colour yellow, also yields up Raskolnikov like a natural secretion, and this vouchsafing process encompasses and transcends the resources both of first- and third-person narrative. To stay with yellow for a moment: we noted a paring-down to the bare bones of yellow water in a yellow glass when Raskolnikov comes to after fainting on his first visit to the police station. An opposite movement occurs with the elements of oppressive heat and smell on the same momentous fourth floor. In the first draft of the scene neither are mentioned. Then, as an afterthought, Dostoevsky wrote "the air was terribly stifling" and "in addition, a smell of wet paint assailed the nostrils." Our final text elaborates this to "the nauseating smell of fresh paint which had been mixed with rancid oil."

Rancid oil is simply right. Hundreds of such details mark Dostoevsky's year-long burst of composition, hour upon hour "without straightening my neck," he said. Thus he caught the police station and the whole city during those few fictional July days when everything except the epilogue happens. And he caught his hero too since a man is (among a million other things—but art concentrates attention) the yellows he sees and tastes, and the evil rancid oil he smells. Also, and perhaps to a greater extent, a man is what he *has* smelt: later in the novel Raskolnikov gives the police-station smell as the reason for the suspicious circumstance of his fainting, which is neither the whole truth nor a straight lie but the blending of the guilty man with the poison of the city.

Crime and Punishment's Petersburg does not produce the murderer with the inevitability shown by the "abstract" city in the novel immediately preceding it, where the Underground Man "was bound to appear in our midst." The draft letter to Katkov merely claims that crimes like this fictional one can be found in the newspapers, and that the fictional murderer has come under the influence of certain half-baked ideas which happen to be in the air at the time. Here, despite life following art with Danilov's double murder, we have an ordinary modest contingent naturalism, and in this area the novel bears out the letter to Katkov. Inevitability, at once psychological and religious, enters (so the letter goes on) after the crime has been committed, in the shape of "the truth of God and the law of nature" which compel Raskolnikov first to be exiled from the humanity he has outraged, and then to confess and accept the public consequences of confession as the only way to become a man among men again. Here we have the apocalyptic naturalism which marks out Dostoevsky absolutely, and in this area too, though we shall find an overreliance upon the epilogue, *Crime and Punishment* follows the Katkov letter while breathing life into its dry and sketchy determinism.

Moreover the novel takes up the remark to Katkov that the criminal "*himself morally demands*" his punishment (which on its own might mean no more than that Dostoevsky had been reading Hegel or popularized Hegel), and builds some marvellous effects upon it. Raskolnikov has of course outraged the human being in himself too; the pad pad pad of the hunter and hunted relationship with Porfiry is intertwined with self-pursuit to the point where the murderer actually makes the running in the second of the three long interviews, arriving unsent-for and demanding interrogation "according to the rules," if interrogation there must be; which leads Porfiry to exclaim: "Good heavens! What do you mean? What is there for me to question you about?" And in the third interview, the net now drawn tight about him, when Porfiry makes a sudden little feint which suggests he won't be accused after all, "Raskolnikov felt a rush of a new kind of fear. The thought that Porfiry believed him innocent suddenly began to frighten him." The reader is both astonished and utterly convinced, as he is later on in the interview when Porfiry plays the dangerous game of saying he has got no real proof, he's going on hunch and "psychology"—so Raskolnikov had better confess. It's up to you, he's saying, to satisfy the hunger which the letter to Katkov and the *Crime and Punishment* notebooks rationalize as the criminal's moral demand.

Porfiry is also asking Raskolnikov to recognize his hunger for what it is. Both he and Sonya Marmeladov, in their separate areas of the novel, impress the need to accept suffering. Now suffering is a vast and many-sided fact of *Crime and Punishment,* as of all mature Dostoevsky—larger than the "loose end" idea of *The Drunks* which produced Marmeladov the marmeladey wallower in abasement and humiliation, the man who seeks suffering and finds it (and so finds satisfaction too) at the bottom of his vodka jug, who screams "I'm loving this!" when his wife pulls him across the room by his hair; and larger than the "out of the practical swim" idea of "A Confession" from which emerges the murderer, the man with something to confess, who doesn't seek suffering but learns, though only in the epilogue, to accept it. Prostitution is the hardest labour in the world, Dostoevsky thought, and Sonya of the yellow ticket who sells her body to buy her family's bread has no loose-end aspect to her suffering. Nor has her consumptive step-mother, Marmeladov's wife, endlessly busy with children and no-home. One can only regard them as victims of other people's loose ends, just as the terrible sustained anxiety of Raskolnikov's mother and sister on his account is the measure of his power to make others suffer as well as himself in that limbo which his friend—his only friend—Razumikhin calls being out of the practical swim. Nastasya, the general maidservant at Raskolnikov's lodging-house, finds him in bed, where he often is nowadays:

"You used to give lessons to children, so you say. Why are you doing nothing now?"

"I am doing—" Raskolnikov began reluctantly and grimly.

"What are you doing?"

"Work."

"What sort of work?"

"Thinking."

Nastasya fairly shook with laughter.

Murderous and anguished work—the thinking that goes on between the rehearsal and the deed itself. This thinking is the mental pulse which registers the single prenatal life of his crime and his punishment. Razumikhin would not have laughed like the jolly Nastasya. Nor would Raskolnikov's poor mother and sister: "but I'm afraid, afraid—oh God he's so strange. He speaks kindly but I'm afraid. What am I afraid of?" We recall that in the notebooks Dostoevsky has Raskolnikov reflect upon his crime and declare he had to commit it to achieve moral development and get himself out of the mess he was in. A comically facile conclusion. Nevertheless he *was* in a festering condition, and the murder *did* induce a crisis. In his exchange with Nastasya he reveals himself an underground man who has wandered into a nineteenth-century naturalistic novel, a bohemian Hamlet. The point of contact with the fable of disembodied consciousness is that thinking has become Raskolnikov's work, it has almost become Raskolnikov, and if he did and were nothing but this work we would have the first part of *Notes from Underground* repeated.

And of course committing the murder is an act of perverse self-assertion, like the Underground Man's notional sticking his tongue out—with the difference that the anti-hero's mind movement breaks no bones, and hurts no feelings except his own. With the murder Raskolnikov erupts into the full glare of the actual, and parts company with his predecessor. But Dostoevsky did not want to surrender the tract of suffering bounded by the sense of being and doing nothing but one's thoughts. The result is Svidrigailov. The notebooks show Svidrigailov developing from a minor into a major character while *Crime and Punishment* was being planned and written, and they show his growth as interdependent with Raskolnikov's final definition. In some early drafts Raskolnikov commits suicide, and the striking thing here is that it's never suggested he does so out of remorse or because he thinks he's going to get caught or even from some vaguer, larger self-loathing. He appears to lose interest in life. He is bored. Sonya asks him, "I don't understand: how will things be for you, how will you marry and have children?"—of course thinking about his estrangement from human kind; and he replies (Dostoevsky's italics): "*I'll get used to it.*"

During the year in which the final version was written it became clear that Raskolnikov must be freed absolutely from suicide and blanket boredom and ripostes like the one about family life which issue out from beneath that boredom. All these are inconsistent with "living life," the two words which are placed between inverted commas and imposed at the level of mere idea upon *Notes from Underground,* but which truly drive Raskolnikov, which are his need to become a man again. Mere existence had not been enough for him, in the epilogue's diagnosis; he has always wanted something more. This wanting teased him on as it happened— contingent naturalism—to murder. Then murder led him inexorably— apocalyptic naturalism—to confess and accept suffering, and acceptance of suffering took him back to mere existence which is living life, neither more nor less. Life is life. It has no outside to it (hence Dostoevsky's ready acceptance of Christ the complete man and his difficulties with God). To theorize about life is not to live. But on the last page of the novel "life had taken the place of dialectics," and Raskolnikov is on his way home.

Meanwhile Svidrigailov has taken over the suicide role, which is to say the blanket boredom has become positively terminal. "You know, I take no particular interest in anything," he tells Raskolnikov musingly on their first encounter; "especially now, I have nothing to occupy me." In his time he has tried a lot of things: card-sharping, prison, wife-thrashing and perhaps wife-murder, child-violation, even good works. He contemplates balloon-travel and a journey to the North Pole. "All my hopes rest on anatomy now, goodness me they do!" "On anatomy?" asks Raskolnikov, understandably mystified. But Svidrigailov ignores the question and starts talking about politics. He puts in a word on behalf of debauchery because "it's an occupation of a sort." Yes and no. The notebooks are beginning to pull him into shape with their "NB. Not an *occupied* man." In fact nothing binds him to life. He pictures eternity as a filthy Russian bathhouse with spiders in the corners, and yet he blows his brains out to send himself there.

It's difficult to avoid making his suicide sound too purposeful. Again the notebooks can be seen moving in the right direction with "*Svidrigailov:* I'm happy to go to America at once, but somehow nobody really wants to." America is his favourite way of talking about the undiscovered country, and it shows that as well as suicide and blanket boredom he has taken over the flavour of Raskolnikov's joke about getting used to family life. Dostoevsky's notebook word "tone" amounts to more than dust and mortar and summer smells; it catches up human beings and entangles them with the city. It's no accident that Svidrigailov is the only one in the novel to handle yellow paper money, just as it's no accident that children are frightened of him and run away "in indescribable terror" because (so we understand in our bones) they smell death on him, or rather the unattachment to life which defeats even Sonya Marmeladov. The girl who has reached the human being in Raskolnikov the murderer is left for the last time by Svidrigailov "bewildered and frightened, and filled with vague and oppressive suspicions." He has just walked out into a spectacular summer storm. As he leaves, she asks him "How can you—how can you go now, in such rain?" "What! All set for America and afraid of the rain!"

America is his bleak private fancy, the loneliest of witticisms. He shares the rain, though, which comes evenhandedly to city and inhabitants, a psychological force like the heat it dispels. The rain brings him an end–of–time vision, solitary as his sense of humour, of flooding cellars and emerging rats. To others it brings relief from the merciless summer heat. Raskolnikov is one of the others, though it's only through the long crime-and-punishment process that he comes to understand this: he had "wanted something more"—more than our mere-existence rain. He had wanted to be a Napoleon and special. In the closing moments of their final interview Porfiry wonders if there's a storm coming—"and it would be no bad thing," he says, "to freshen the air"; which is a literal rephrasing of the metaphorical "All you want now is air, air, air!" with which he presses home his argument for confession and acceptance of suffering, and for life.

Porfiry's words have a heightened transpersonal effect because Svidrigailov has just told Raskolnikov the same thing. "Ah, Rodion Romanovich," he says completely out of the blue, "what every man needs is air, air, air! That above all!" He doesn't exclude himself. Balloon-travel, debauchery, card-sharping and so forth are frustrated struggles for air, and he knows it. When eavesdropping (a vicarious ghost-life he goes in for), he hears Raskolnikov tell Sonya about the crime, and later, without openly referring to it, the potential suicide twits the actual murderer: "Well, you can certainly do a lot."

The irony of murder as doing a lot—doing *anything*—bears the stamp of Svidrigailov. He is probably a murderer himself; the lightmindedness of his retrospective half-confirmations and half-denials is oddly disgusting; and for him killing people is no more doing something than sleeping with little girls or setting off for the North Pole. It's just another struggle for air, for living life. He recognizes in Raskolnikov a fellow-struggler, and repeatedly he says that the two of them are birds of a feather; but he also bids him farewell with a pointed "You to the right and I to the left, or the other way round if you like" towards the end of their final meeting, because setting off for America, unlike the North Pole, while it may or may not amount to doing anything (*Crime and Punishment* doesn't raise the question) marks a parting of their ways. In Svidrigailov's America there is no air to struggle for, and no rain to soften hearts and freshen cities and give the excluded (or self-excluding) man occasion for jokes about fear and death.

Most people breathe naturally, they don't struggle for air. In the Underground Man's sick yet piercing analysis, most people are roadbuilders, instinctively being somebody, doing something, going somewhere. Not so the antihero himself paralysed by the disease of hyperconsciousness in abstract Petersburg. And not so Svidrigailov and Raskolnikov, both hyperconscious men, and both (as we shall see) linked by their condition to the city which Peter the Great pondered over and then ordered to be built. Svidrigailov's answer, when Raskolnikov asks him "Why don't you see a doctor?" is that he doesn't need to be told he's ill. It doesn't follow that he knows what the matter is—"honestly, though, I don't know what's wrong with me," he adds. He hasn't got the underground man's bodiless analytic clarity. He only knows that he needs air and can't get it; a state evinced by his terminal boredom, and by single sovereign descriptive strokes like the fact that his eyes are "a little too blue," leaving the reader to imagine a pair of empty summer-sky souls, very bright and staring in pain.

One of the marvels of *Crime and Punishment* is its clear distinguishing, untainted by clinical knowingness, of Svidrigailov's and Raskolnikov's ways of being (as the saying is) not with us. Svidrigailov appears not to notice insults and rudenesses. Nothing signifies for him, yet he seizes on details with a toneless precision, almost pendantry: when Raskolnikov calls him a gambler he says he is actually a card-sharper. Observing Raskolnikov wince at the idea of eternity as a bathhouse, he murmurs "with a vague smile" that he would certainly have made it like that himself. He suggests that behind Raskolnikov's sister's loathing of him there lurks attraction, and he states flatly that she and his own wife were once in love with each other; and perhaps he is right. Ghosts visit him, he says. He frequents a seedy restaurant—"You see this wretched tavern I spend all my time in, and I enjoy it, or rather it's not that I really enjoy it, but one must have somewhere to perch": this is the form which the Dostoevsky no-home takes with him, likewise the transpersonal motif first voiced by Marmeladov in this novel, that a man must have somewhere to go. He is absent yet meticulous, paying for a missing drink-shop teaspoon which has nothing to do with him, and spending a long time in the "interesting occupation" of trying to catch a fly. (Recall "not an *occupied* man" from the notebooks. And recall Kafka on incidental madness in Dostoevsky; it's not just the children whom Svidrigailov terrifies.)

Raskolnikov is not with us either, but in the novel's final text he could not have done or said any of the things I have just mentioned. Even his way of throwing his money about, what he has of it, is immediately distinguishable from Svidrigailov's, while with both of them money is the very image of merely imputed and therefore reversible value in a loose-end world: "You to the right and I to the left, or the other way round if you like." Cocooned in false-Napoleonic narcissism he reads about his own deed in the newspapers. He goes in for a sort of hall-of-mirrors self-impersonation, telling people how he would have done the murder if he had done it (which he has). His crime-and-punishment existence is a process of endless self-monitoring:

> What Razumikhin had just said about Porfiry also disturbed him.
>
> "I'll have to play the sick man act with him too," he thought, white in the face, his heart pounding, "and I'll have to do it naturally. But the most natural thing of all would be to do nothing. *Make a point* of doing nothing. No, *making a point* would be unnatural again. Oh well, it depends how things turn out—we'll see—soon enough—is it a good idea to go there or not? The moth flies into the flame of her own accord. My heart's pounding, and that's bad!"

A normalizing and fleshing-out of Mr Golyadkin deciding to adopt a passive role. And the details of Raskolnikov's alienation show Dostoevsky at his most unrelentingly careful and sensitive. In another passage our final text reads "His words were as if meant for himself, but he spoke them aloud, and he continued for some time to look at his sister like a man perplexed." The first draft has "he thought to himself" but nothing about the sister. The second draft introduces the sister and cuts the thinking to himself. The magazine text brings in the paradox of public and yet *as if* private utterance: "His words were as if spoken to himself, but he spoke them aloud, and he continued for some time to look at his sister like a man perplexed." And that is how the passage appeared in volume form, in the editions of 1867 and 1870. But in 1877, the last text overseen by the novelist, "as if spoken to himself" becomes "as if meant for himself," shifting and refining nuance while involving the change of a single word in Russian, and enabling the artist to get at last the effect he had been working to-wards.

The naturalness of doing nothing. The unnaturalness of making a point of doing nothing. These are underground and pre-Siberian thoughts. But a new sort of humour has arrived: witness the exquisite dew-drop exchange between Svidrigailov and Raskolnikov:

> "Incidentally, do you believe in ghosts?"
> "What kind of ghosts?"
> "Ordinary ghosts, of course."

And with the young doctor who tries to help Raskolnikov, the voice of the underground man has become more accessibly funny: "I admit there's scarcely such a thing as a normal human being. You might find one in tens or perhaps hundreds of thousands, but even he will turn out a rather feeble specimen."

We all limp, more or less, was the antihero's way of putting it, and for him all consciousness was a disease. His own hyperconsciousness, the disease in an acute form, he considered a product of nineteenth-century civilization, rendered yet more virulent by the "abstract and intentional city" he lived in. This tight argument becomes relaxed and humanized in *Crime and Punishment*. The hyperconscious Double Act in which Svidrigailov's terminal boredom plays opposite the greedy, theoretical self-assertion of Raskolnikov's wanting "something more" than "mere existence," becomes grounded in suicide and murder; and the Petersburg where these things happen gains a fuzzy-edged documentary aspect which never comes anywhere near dominating the novel, but which is there. Once and once only a finger is placed, by Svidrigailov appropriately, on the fact that Peter's city turns people odd. He mentions the climate, but without filling in the summer smells of this novel, or the fog and white nights and wet snow of others. And he observes in a flat parajournalistic way that Petersburg is "the administrative centre of all Russia." This makes it a city of arrivers. Some come like Marmeladov to get a job on the appropriate rung of the bureaucratic ladder. Others are in search of justice, "with a petition to some Minister." Others again, like Mr Luzhin, Dunya Raskolnikov's middle-aged suitor, want to make a lot of money: there's a Dick Whittington side to Petersburg. Speaking for himself, Svidrigailov says he is after the women, which isn't untrue but we know what it's worth. Raskolnikov has been here three years. He arrived from the deep country to attend university. His friend Razumikhin, a truthful witness, has known him for eighteen months. Razumikhin himself may or may not have come from the country, but he is certainly a member of the floating, unbelonging population of students and ex-students, and he records in simple puzzlement that Raskolnikov has been growing increasingly moody and suspicious and introverted; "he has no time for anything, people are always in his way, and yet he lies about and does nothing"—a confirming echo of Raskolnikov on his bed telling Nastasya the maid that he is working, by which he means thinking. His mind's not right. Petersburg encourages his vicious loose-end tendency, as it teases Svidrigailov with phantom images of what is would be like to be an occupied man. Raskolnikov's "incomplete smile" is the index of those "half-baked" (literally, "incomplete") ideas which Dostoevsky writes about in the letter to Katkov.

IV

Among *Crime and Punishment*'s major characters only Porfiry the detective is in no sense an arriver. It will appear mechanical, when plucked out of the huge and vital narrative flow, that Dostoevsky has given him "a sickly dark yellow complexion" as a mark of his belonging to Petersburg. Nevertheless he does possess a yellow face as opposed to lodging in a yellow room, or handling yellow money, or being issued (the bureaucracy!) with a yellow ticket. He also belongs for the reason suggested by Svidrigailov; Petersburg is the administrative centre of Russia, and Porfiry occupies his position there as an official examining magistrate within the metropolitan and national legal system.

Therefore he has a public front and function as well as an unhealthy yellow human face. It's his job to bring the murderer of the old moneylender and her sister to justice. The job occupies him, as Svidrigailov would say; it involves both the man and the salaried magistrate, and it defines the part played by Porfiry in the apocalyptic naturalism of the crime-and-punishment process. But what is there for Porfiry to do? We have just caught Raskolnikov saying to himself that the moth seeks the candle-flame, and Porfiry says similar things aloud; while behind both of them Dostoevsky is telling Katkov that the murderer demands punishment and bends to an inexorable divine and human law when he gives himself up. At one level, as in all picturings of God's rule and man's free will, there is nothing for Porfiry to do; he just has to sit and wait, which he is good at. And at another level he has to know and play every trick of the detective's trade, which he is good at too.

Cat and mouse has no less force, in this fated relationship, than moth and candle-flame. "I won't allow myself to be tortured," Raskolnikov tells

Porfiry, but our sense of their three long encounters is that there's nothing either of them can do about it. In a single serpentine sentence Porfiry seems to dissolve into his own prose, showering Raskolnikov with a patter of tiny verbal blows as if exercising the Russian particle for its own sake (*nu da uzh*), telling him that he considers him "quite incapable" of committing suicide, and in the same breath to leave "a short circumstantial note" if he does. This, in the blood and bone of the novel, is how the doubleness—the two levels—appears, in which all is destined and anything can happen. It might be objected that the doubleness is just a trick of Porfiry's. But this wouldn't match up to the greatness of the Porfiry–Raskolnikov scenes. It isn't *just* a trick. And it isn't just *Porfiry's* trick. Life in the guise of the crime-and-punishment process snatches up hunter and hunted into the contradictions and cruelties and deceits and frailties which are, in a word, life—not the whole of life of course, but life. Porfiry misquotes Raskolnikov back at himself. He commends him for the wit and wisdom of things he hasn't said. He tacks on tendentious continuations to things Raskolnikov has said. He suggests that he's got no evidence, then that he's got some evidence, then both at once: "There's nothing here, precisely nothing, perhaps absolutely nothing"—the torture tune. Surrounded by "government furniture of polished yellow wood," he proffers blandishing diminutives; "how about a spot of open window?" (*okoshechko*) he asks the ready fainter. He drops, or there happen to be dropped, sore words like "Napoleon" and "axe" into his discourse. He scrambles his own identity as a man and magistrate: "Do you suppose I didn't come to search your room at the time? I did, I did—ha, ha!—I was here when you were lying ill in bed. Not officially, and not in my own person, but I was here."

What is Raskolnikov supposed to make of that? Or the reader? Or Porfiry himself? *Crime and Punishment* is a ghostly book in which all three—murderer, detective, reader—tiptoe mentally round dubitable presences and absences, and create between themselves strange large silences. Again and again the murder of Lizaveta is ignored. And yet Raskolnikov's greater enormity is that having forgotten to bolt the door after killing the money-lender he is surprised by her half-sister, the woman who mends linen and has mended his in her time, apparently always pregnant, through simplicity, not waywardness, meek-eyed though "she looks like a soldier dressed up as a woman" (who but Dostoevsky!) and Raskolnikov kills Lizaveta too. Since Porfiry wants to break Raskolnikov, why doesn't he exploit Lizaveta's murder? Raskolnikov is no moral idiot. He recognizes an atrocity when he commits one. Equally, why is it not pointed up that philanthropic murder and the Napoleonic idea and all other theorizing come unstuck here?

There seems no reason, and the very business of raising such questions is itself part of a widespread collusive conjuring of absences and of whole worlds of what might have been. The fact remains that Porfiry does break, or tame, Raskolnikov, and that an enterprise lucid in prospect becomes fogbound by the chance which brings Lizaveta home unexpectedly. She, the simple mender and dealer in second-hand clothes, happens to return as she happens to keep getting pregnant—and what fuller and neater manifestation of chance than that, than conceiving and being conceived?

Lizaveta's final outrage is inflicted by a man who almost cleaves her head in two. Raskolnikov uses the blade of his axe on her, whereas he has just used the back of it on the older woman, crushing her skull. Again these things happen as they do happen, the magic narrative containing spur-of-the-moment impulse within trancelike inevitability. Readers are at one, levels of sophistication vanish, in those cinematic sequences on stairs and landings, where footsteps echo and distant doors slam, and in a flat below two workmen fool about and daub each other with paint. We all see with one pair of eyes, Raskolnikov's, when the visual field narrows upon the back of an old woman's head, her hair "thick with grease, twisted into a rat's-tail plait and gathered up under what was left of a broken horn comb which stuck out at the nape of her neck."

That broken comb exemplifies the apparently inexhaustible strength of the novel's flotsam, its disjunctive detail which makes nevertheless for tonal coherence. The painters downstairs, skylarking on the fringe of the main action, celebrate (though they would be surprised to hear it) the living life which was, I said, merely imposed on *Notes from Underground,* but which now surrounds both crime and punishment and makes the whole novel responsive like a touched spider's web. Nastasya the maid has only to hand Raskolnikov a bowl of soup for his mental structures to be set trembling in their unrealism. Lizaveta once mended his clothes: when we puzzle over the chance-induced actuality of her murder being so largely left to *speak for itself* we are creating a false problem by the inertness of our own metaphor. "Didn't I live just now?" Raskolnikov asks himself after he has helped the Marmeladov family and been in contact with little children. Other existences rub off on him, as can be shown at the grammatical level when he overhears a student and an army officer discussing the money-lender. "I would kill that damned old woman without a single twinge of conscience," says the former, and proceeds to give his reasons. "Here you are talking and holding forth," says the latter, "but tell me this:

are you going to kill the old woman *yourself*?" Translators have "would you kill?" here, but Dostoevsky uses the future tense for the officer, whereas the student's "I would kill" is genuinely in the conditional. This distinction should be preserved (even though the Russian verb is not quite square with the English), since it belongs to the novel's overall life-against-logic argument: in theory the student would kill her, but in fact he won't. "Of course not!" he tells the army officer, and that's the end of it.

Acting by theory, Raskolnikov does kill her, and life impinges. The two painters downstairs impinge—directly through their crazy behaviour arousing suspicion against themselves, and indirectly through Porfiry. Porfiry uses them to try and catch Raskolnikov out. They were working in a flat below the old money-lender's at the time of the murder, but not at the time of the "rehearsal" three days earlier. Raskolnikov has admitted to visiting the old woman on the first occasion but of course not on the second. Pretending to be worried about the painters and the incriminating evidence against them—"It's very, very important for them!"—Porfiry asks Raskolnikov if he has any recollection of passing an open door on the lower landing and seeing two men at work inside. For a split second Raskolnikov is thrown. His attention has been decoyed. He gropes mentally, "straining every nerve in an agonised attempt to divine as quickly as possible where the trap lay." And then he sees it, and the moment is successfully negotiated.

Porfiry's bait for Raskolnikov ("a precious question" Dostoevsky calls this dangled interrogative hook in his notebooks) holds a different but equally potent fascination for the reader, instancing the story's inexorable grip and the virtuosity of the examining magistrate at work. Porfiry is, as we say, very human. He smokes too much and is overweight, altogether in poor physical shape. This simply goes along with his being the archetypal great detective, and even with Dostoevsky making him a vehicle for the airing of central thematic issues. In their third and last encounter Porfiry tells Raskolnikov that what he needs more than anything is somebody to be—"life and a definite position." This echoes the statement in their second encounter that he, Porfiry, has no intention of making an immediate arrest because by doing so he would give the murderer somebody to be: "I'd give him, so to say, a definite position, I'd give him psychological definition and peace." Peace! The out-of-the-practical-swim ex-student, ex-teacher, the worker at thinking in bed, would be able to call himself an arrested man! We think back to the antihero of *Notes from Underground* lamenting that he can't even call himself a lazy man, and we think sideways to Svidrigailov: "Believe me, if only I were something; a landowner, say, or a father, a cavalry officer, a photographer, a journalist say—but I'm nothing, I've no speciality." He too ("birds of a feather") has nobody to be, and the ice-cold comedy of his father/photographer/landowner *mélange* projects the disjunctive genius of *Crime and Punishment* on yet another plane.

In any case, says Porfiry, there is no need to lock Raskolnikov up, because "you won't run away." He has nowhere to run to, nowhere, absolutely nowhere, to go. His crime has brought him to the extremity which Marmeladov was telling him about and tasting at the bottom of his own vodka jug in the opening pages of the novel. Moreover, Porfiry adds, "what will you run away with?" An amazing stroke. Raskolnikov is Mr Naked done again. Porfiry means that he doesn't really believe in his theory; to wonder if he is a Napoleon is to prove to himself that he isn't. It is to steal his own clothes, and by the time he comes to Sonya to confess, the Napoleonic idea is already crumbling into wanting to dare or something even vaguer.

And nobody else can be a Napoleon either. A Napoleon is a nonperson, a "generalhuman"; and although the word doesn't appear in *Crime and Punishment* itself, the notebooks make the point that one can't just live "the general life of humanity." In this general-human life there would be "nothing whatever to do," the notebook continues. Napoleon himself had plenty to do, but *a* Napoleon is a member of a conceptual class of people who are like each other; and likeness, the "unseemly likeness" of *The Double,* is fraught throughout Dostoevsky. When Raskolnikov goes to Sonya to declare himself, she implores him to tell her "straight out—without examples." She doesn't want to know what he's *like.* She wants to know *him,* in his unique humanity.

Which also means his shared humanity. "But how," she cries, "how can you live without human society?" (literally, "without a human being"). She knows he can't, as does Porfiry who will soon rephrase her question in statement form: "*You can't get on without us.*" His typically unspecific and floated "*us*" is the human family which Raskolnikov must rejoin, and he can't rejoin it without accepting suffering. Both Sonya and Porfiry tell him so.

The words come easier from Porfiry who speaks for public justice than from Sonya on whom falls the main and mystic burden of creative, regenerative suffering. Marmeladov's huge notebook gesture towards Christ and the Russian people and suffering constitutes one warning that Dostoevsky was, at one stage, after something too big or too difficult or perhaps simply wrong for *Crime and Punishment;* and Sonya's declaration,

again in the notebooks, makes a second: "The Russian people have always
suffered like Christ, says Sonya." In the novel itself we meet the Russian
people, the folk, only once, and then as inflictors of suffering, in Raskolnikov's half-dream (which is also half-memory) of a little mare being tortured and finally clubbed to death by drunken peasants. Mrs Marmeladov's death is very like an animal's, like this mare's: "Her bloodless,
yellow, wasted face dropped back, her mouth opened, her legs straight-
ened convulsively. She heaved a deep, deep sigh and died." The whole
novel reeks of pain. We mustn't think of its Petersburg crowds as the folk
(*narod*); they are a medley of exploiters and exploited, above all of arrivers
and non-belongers. When, on his final journey to the police station,
Raskolnikov kneels down in the middle of the Haymarket and kisses "the
earth, the filthy earth" (*zemlya*) as Sonya has bidden, it is entirely calculated by Dostoevsky that a tipsy artisan should laugh at the strange young
man who "is bowing down to the whole world and is kissing the capital
city of St Petersburg and its soil" (*grunt,* the German *Grund*). This has no
more to do with Christ and regenerative suffering than Dr Rutenspitz telling Mr Golyadkin that *Licht* will be provided for him where he's going at
the end of *The Double*.

But in the epilogue, as opposed to the body of *Crime and Punishment,*
people don't torture animals or bear the mark of Peter the German. We
are back in the world of the Dead House, of simple Russian convicts and
Sorrel the horse, their pride and joy. In effect Dostoevsky is revisiting his
own fortress prison at Omsk. Raskolnikov is here, serving an eight-year
sentence. He has got off lightly: we learn with mildly comic surprise of
mitigating circumstances: he had been good to a consumptive fellow student, and he had saved two children from a blazing house, getting burnt
himself while doing so.

More important, and very surprising, we are told that "he did not repent of his crime." So his rallying himself to enter the police station "*as a
man*" and confess was not the acceptance of suffering which Sonya and
Porfiry both—but separately—urged him towards. Or rather, it was not
yet that acceptance, something in Raskolnikov remained obdurate. Prison
finds him longing to feel contrite, to feel he deserves his punishment, but
only able to believe he has committed "a simple *blunder* which might have
happened to anybody." Then, as the notebooks put it, "Sonya and love
broke him." On the same page we read about a vision of Christ and a
seeking forgiveness of the common people—two ideas which were abandoned. And it should be noted that the actual breaking point for Raskolnikov in the novel is the illness which induces his apocalyptic science-fiction

nightmare of germs and *Possessed*-type madness and destruction, bringing him literally to Sonya's feet and both of them to "the dawn of a new future, of a full resurrection into a new life" which will be the subject of another story.

So having laid the weight of mystic, creative suffering on Sonya, the novel proceeds to hive it off into its own epilogue where all strains and difficulties are waved away. What the Sonya of the novel has to do with Christ and resurrection and creative suffering remains fleeting and indirect, though no less wonderful for that. In the original version, now lost, of the chapter in which she reads to Raskolnikov the gospel story of the raising of Lazarus, Dostoevsky intended and wrote a head-on debate about Christianity; but his publishers refused to print it. The novelist was very distressed. And yet he took no steps to reintroduce it in later editions. I believe he came to see it would not do. As with the censored Christian argument in *Notes from Underground,* I believe an unfathomable good luck wearing the face of bad luck was on his side at the start. If Raskolnikov was to have mounted an assault of something like Grand Inquisitor proportions, if he was to have expatiated on the whole God business not being worth the pain of one misused child, then the time wasn't ripe; we must wait for Ivan Karamazov. And if Sonya was to have replied to him, what could she have said? No more than the answer she gave in the *Crime and Punishment* which did get printed, to the not quite taunting question "And what does God do for you?"

"He does everything," she says, but there is no debate. Sonya is the church-slavonic "daughter" (*dshcher*) whom Marmeladov introduces in his pub tirade. God will call her to Him on the Day of Judgment, asking "Where is the daughter who had pity on her earthly father, the filthy drunkard, and was undismayed by his beastliness?" There must be many who are touched to the heart by that phrase "earthly father" and yet who don't believe a word of the novel's religion; just as, and more obviously, Raskolnikov's kissing the dirt in the middle of the Haymarket doesn't stand or fall by Dostoevsky's Soil Philosophy. For the earth and the filth are the realized human stuff of the book. Not, of course, all its human stuff; when Dostoevsky told his biographer that the task of his own deeper realism was "to find the human in the human being," he meant there is more to us than filthy earth, and this "more" must be found. In extremity, with nowhere to go, and not even a believed theory to wear or hold his mind's hand ("what will you run away with?"), Raskolnikov turns to Sonya; "it was to her, Sonya, that he first went with his confession; when he felt the need of a human being, he sought the human being in her"—

which does indeed isolate for a moment, and emphasize, the mystic business of his alienation from the human family; and for this moment the dross (as it were) of Sonya and of Raskolnikov is withheld; the god in his humanity is looking for the god in hers.

But the Raskolnikov of the notebooks who joked grimly about getting used to being married and having children will do that average and earthy thing, though in a different spirit; and in another story, as the epilogue tells us. The Raskolnikov of *Crime and Punishment* has got *unused* to everything; all the calm pressures of habit are denied him, his punishment has begun. And the Sonya of the novel is very slightly indicated. She is little more than her blue eyes and green shawl, the blue and the green undismayed by the yellows and reds of the book, as the girl is by her father.

He, the loose-end, filthy-earth drunkard, introduces the shawl as he does so many motifs. He describes how Sonya is driven out onto the streets by her step-mother's gibe—"Why not? What is there to preserve so carefully?"—and returns and lays thirty roubles on the table.

> "She looked at her step-mother but uttered not a single word; she simply picked up our big *drap-de-dames* green shawl (it's a shawl we all use, a *drap-de-dames* one), and covered her head and face entirely with it and lay down on the bed with her face to the wall, and her little shoulders and her whole body were trembling."

His "which we all use" is authorially bold. We are never told what use Marmeladov might have had for the shawl. But, "We are one, we live as one," says Sonya in the Lazarus chapter, and that is much bolder. Greater disunity than that of the Marmeladov non-home can scarcely be imagined. I've just mentioned the taunt that drives Sonya to prostitution. Members of the family are sleeping in three different places. Even the father's funeral feast explodes in chaos—the classic Dostoevsky *skandal*. And yet, while God doing everything for Sonya remains shielded by her faith, the green shawl keeps cropping up through the novel for all to see. She puts it on to follow Raskolnikov on his final journey to the police station, and through his mind flashes the thought that this is the shawl Marmeladov referred to in the pub as "the family one." Actually Marmeladov said "which we all use." Dostoevsky will have remembered that; it is one of those overlapping cumulations, sameness with difference, which reveal simultaneously the closeness of his workmanship and his imagination's bias.

Our last sight is of the shawl flitting about among the convicts in Siberia: not altogether happy, like many things in the epilogue. Again it should be seen as close and calculated that the shawl which wraps the head in shame at first, becomes at last a green emblem of mercy. And yet the effective place of this life-soiled object is in the body of the book, nourishing the reality of the whole Marmeladov set-up, like the children's washed day-clothes drying overnight. For there are no spare things. On second thoughts there is nothing surprising in "which we all use"; how could it be otherwise in a *family* like the Marmeladov's?

And Sonya's "We are one, we live as one," while it remains authorially bold, has nothing to fear at the hands of readers quick to sniff out dogma. *Crime and Punishment* naturalizes the mystic brazenness of Sonya's statement, as it does Porfiry's "*You can't get on without us.*" Parajournalism, creating to one side of the actual, seems to me the nub here. When Svidrigailov and Porfiry, who never meet—bold again—and who have nothing to do with each other, both tell Raskolnikov that a man needs air, my business is to try and suggest how it is that Dostoevsky's reader finds himself in immediate dual touch with a Petersburg July day and a universal truth.

He senses, too, that the actual has more than one side to it. Thus when the girl secretary who was to become Dostoevsky's wife rang the bell of his flat for the first time, the door was opened by an elderly woman servant with a green shawl thrown over her shoulders. Anna Grigorevna had been reading *Crime and Punishment* in the magazine *Russian Herald,* and she thought she recognized the object "which played such a big part in the Marmeladov family." No doubt she did. And soon afterwards, in the first week of their marriage, Dostoevsky showed her the stone under which Raskolnikov hid the stuff he had taken from the old money-lender. She asked her husband what had brought him—Dostoevsky—to this deserted yard. He replied, "The reason that does in fact bring people to secluded places." Now that's our man.

Carnival and Space in *Crime and Punishment*

Mikhail Bakhtin

Carnivalization is not an external and immobile schema which is imposed upon ready-made content; it is, rather, an extraordinarily flexible form of artistic visualization, a peculiar sort of heuristic principle making possible the discovery of new and as yet unseen things. By *relativizing* all that was externally stable, set and ready-made, carnivalization with its pathos of change and renewal permitted Dostoevsky to penetrate into the deepest layers of man and human relationships. It proved remarkably productive as a means for capturing in art the developing relationships under capitalism, at a time when previous forms of life, moral principles and beliefs were being turned into "rotten cords" and the previously concealed, ambivalent, and unfinalized nature of man and human *thought* was being nakedly exposed. Not only people and their actions but even *ideas* had broken out of their self-enclosed hierarchical nesting places and had begun to collide in the familiar contact of "absolute" (that is, completely unlimited) dialogue. Capitalism, similar to that "pander" Socrates on the market square of Athens, brings together people and ideas. In all of Dostoevsky's novels, beginning with *Crime and Punishment,* there is a consistent *carnivalization* of dialogue.

We find other instances of carnivalization in *Crime and Punishment.* Everything in this novel—the fates of people, their experiences and ideas—is pushed to its boundaries, everything is prepared, as it were, to pass over into its opposite (but not, of course, in the abstractly dialectical sense), ev-

From *Problems of Dostoevsky's Poetics,* edited and translated by Caryl Emerson. © 1984 by the University of Minnesota. University of Minnesota Press, 1984.

erything is taken to the extreme, to its outermost limit. There is nothing in the novel that could become stabilized, nothing that could justifiably relax within itself, enter the ordinary flow of biographical time and develop in it (the possibility of such a development for Razumikhin and Dounia is only indicated by Dostoevsky at the end of the novel, but of course he does not show it; such life lies outside his artistic world). Everything requires change and rebirth. Everything is shown in a moment of unfinalized transition.

It is characteristic that the very setting for the action of the novel—*Petersburg* (its role in the novel is enormous)—is on the borderline between existence and nonexistence, reality and phantasmagoria, always on the verge of dissipating like the fog and vanishing. Petersburg too is devoid, as it were, of any internal grounds for justifiable stabilization; it too is on the threshold.

The sources of carnivalization for *Crime and Punishment* are no longer provided by Gogol. We feel here in part a Balzacian type of carnivalization, and in part elements of the social-adventure novel (Soulié and Sue). But perhaps the most vital and profound source of carnivalization for this novel was Pushkin's *Queen of Spades*.

We shall pause for analysis on only one small episode of the novel, which will permit us to investigate several important characteristics of carnivalization in Dostoevsky, and at the same time clarify our claim concerning Pushkin's influence.

After the first meeting with Porfiry and the appearance of the mysterious artisan with his one word, "Murderer!" Raskolnikov has a *dream* in which he *again* commits the murder of the old woman. We quote the end of this dream:

> He stood over her. "She is afraid," he thought. He stealthily took the axe from the noose and struck her one blow, then another on the skull. But strange to say she did not stir, as though she were made of wood. He was frightened, bent down nearer and tried to look at her; but she, too, bent her head lower. He bent right down to the ground and peeped up into her face from below, he peeped and turned cold with horror; the old woman was sitting and *laughing, shaking with noiseless laughter,* doing her utmost that he should not hear it. Suddenly he fancied that the door from the bedroom was opened a little and that there was *laughter* and whispering within. He was overcome with frenzy and he began hitting the old woman on the

head with all his force, but at every blow of the axe and the *laughter* and whispering from the bedroom *grew louder* and the old woman was simply shaking with mirth. He was rushing away, but the *passage was full of people, the doors* of the flats stood open and *on the landing, on the stairs* and everywhere below there were people, rows of heads, *all looking,* but huddled together in silence and expectation. Something gripped his heart, his legs were rooted to the spot, they would not move. . . . He tried to scream and woke up.

(part 3, chap. 6)

Several points are of interest here.

1. The first point is already familiar to us: the fantastic logic of dreams employed here by Dostoevsky. We recall his words: "you *leap over* space and time, *over all laws of life and reason,* and only pause where your *heart's desire* bids you pause" ("Dream of a Ridiculous Man"). This same dream logic made it possible to create here the image of a *laughing murdered old woman, to combine laughter with death and murder.* But this is also made possible by the ambivalent logic of carnival. Before us is a typical carnival combination.

The image of the laughing old woman in Dostoevsky echoes Pushkin's image of the old Countess winking from the coffin, and the winking Queen of Spades on the card (the Queen of Spades is, incidentally, a *carnival double* of the old Countess). We have here a *fundamental* resonance between two images and not a chance external similarity, for it occurs against the background of a general resonance between these two works (*The Queen of Spades* and *Crime and Punishment*). This is a resonance both in the atmosphere of images and in the basic content of ideas: "Napoleonism" on the specific terrain of early Russian capitalism. In both works this concretely historical phenomenon receives a second *carnivalistic plane,* one which recedes into infinite semantic space. The motivation for these two echoing images (the laughing dead woman) is also similar: in Pushkin it is *insanity,* in Dostoevsky, the *delirious dream.*

2. In Raskolnikov's dream it is not only the murdered woman who laughs (in the dream, to be sure, it proves impossible to murder her). Other people are also laughing, elsewhere in the apartment, in the bedroom, and they laugh louder and louder. Then a crowd appears, a multitude of people on the *stairway* and *down below* as well, and in relation to this crowd passing *below,* Raskolnikov is located at the *top of the stairs.* Before us is the image of communal ridicule on the public square decrowning

a carnival king-pretender. The public square is a symbol of the communal
performance, and at the end of the novel, Raskolnikov, before going to
give himself up at the police station, comes out on the square and bows
low to the earth before the whole people. This communal decrowning,
which "came to Raskolnikov's heart" in a dream, has no *direct* echo in the
The Queen of Spades, but a distant echo is nevertheless there: Hermann's
fainting spell in the presence of the people at the Countess's grave. A fuller
echo of Raskolnikov's dream can be found in another of Pushkin's works,
Boris Godunov. We have in mind the thrice-recurring prophetic *dream* of
the Pretender (the scene in the cell of Chudovo Monastery):

> I dreamed I climbed a *crooked stair* that led
> Up to a tower, and there upon that *height*
> I stood, where Moscow like an ant hill lay
> *Under* my feet, and in the *marketplace*
> The *people* stared and pointed at me *laughing;*
> *I felt ashamed, a trembling overcame me,*
> I fell headfirst, and in that fall I woke.

Here is the same carnival logic of self-appointed *elevation,* the communal act of comic *decrowning on the public square,* and a falling *downward.*

3. In Raskolnikov's dream, *space* assumes additional significance in
the overall symbol-system of carnival. *Up, down,* the *stairway,* the *threshold,* the *foyer,* the *landing* take on the meaning of a "point" where *crisis,*
radical change, an unexpected turn of fate takes place, where decisions are
made, where the forbidden line is overstepped, where one is renewed or
perishes.

Action in Dostoevsky's works occurs primarily at these "points." The
interior spaces of a house or of rooms, spaces distant from the boundaries,
that is from the threshold, are almost never used by Dostoevsky, except
of course for scenes of scandals and decrownings, when interior space (the
drawing room or the hall) becomes a substitute for the public square. Dostoevsky "leaps over" all that is comfortably habitable, well-arranged and
stable, all that is far from the threshold, because the life that he portrays
does not take place in that sort of space. Dostoevsky was least of all an
estate-home-room-apartment-family writer. In comfortably habitable interior space, far from the threshold, people live a biographical life in biographical time: they are born, they pass through childhood and youth,
they marry, give birth to children, die. This biographical time Dostoevsky
also "leaps over." On the threshold and on the square the only time possible is *crisis time,* in which a *moment* is equal to years, decades, even to a
"billion years" (as in the "Dream of a Ridiculous Man").

If we now turn from Raskolnikov's *dream* to what happens in the waking life of the novel, we will be persuaded that the threshold and its substitutes are the fundamental "points" of action in the novel.

First of all, Raskolnikov lives, in essence, on a threshold: his narrow room, a "coffin" (a carnival symbol here) opens directly onto the *landing of the staircase,* and he never locks his door, even when he goes out (that is, his room is unenclosed interior space). In this "coffin" it is impossible to live a biographical life—here one can experience only crisis, make ultimate decisions, die or be reborn (as in the coffins of "Bobok" or the coffin of the Ridiculous Man). Marmeladov's family lives on the threshold as well, in a walk-through room leading directly onto a staircase (here, on the threshold, while bringing home the drunken Marmeladov, Raskolnikov meets the members of the family for the first time). Raskolnikov experiences terrible moments at the threshold of the murdered pawnbroker's when, on the other side of the door, on the stairway landing, her visitors stand and tug at the bell. It is to this place that he returns and himself rings the bell, in order to relive those moments. The scene of his half-confession to Razumikhin takes place on the threshold in the corridor by a lamp, without words, only in glances. On the threshold, near the doors leading to a neighboring apartment, his conversations with Sonya occur (with Svidrigailov eavesdropping on the other side of the door). There is certainly no need to enumerate further all the "acts" that take place on the threshold, near the threshold, or that are permeated with the living sensation of threshold in this novel.

The threshold, the foyer, the corridor, the landing, the stairway, its steps, doors opening onto the stairway, gates to front and back yards, and beyond these, the city: squares, streets, facades, taverns, dens, bridges, gutters. This is the space of the novel. And in fact absolutely nothing here ever loses touch with the threshold, there is no interior of drawing rooms, dining rooms, halls, studios, bedrooms where biographical life unfolds and where events take place in the novels of writers such as Turgenev, Tolstoy, and Goncharov. Of course, we can uncover just such an organization of space in Dostoevsky's other works as well.

Chronology

1821 Fyodor Mikailovich Dostoevsky born October 30 in a Moscow hospital for the poor, where his father was a resident surgeon.

1837 Death of Dostoevsky's mother.

1838 Dostoevsky enters military engineering school in St. Petersburg.

1839 In the wake of increasingly harsh and abusive treatment, Dostoevsky believed, the serfs on Dostoevsky's father's estate castrate and murder their master. Recent evidence, however, casts doubt on the circumstances of his father's death.

1843 Dostoevsky finishes engineering course; joins engineering department of the War Ministry.

1844 Resigns from his post. Publishes his translation of *Eugenie Grandet*.

1845 Finishes his first novel, *Poor Folk,* which wins the acclaim of radical critic Belinsky.

1846 *Poor Folk* published in *St. Petersburg Miscellany*. *The Double* published in *Notes from the Fatherland* two weeks later.

1847 "A Novel in Nine Letters" published in *The Contemporary*. Dostoevsky frequents meetings of the Petrashevsky circle, a clandestine society of progressive thinkers. Publishes pamphlets in the *St. Petersburg Chronicle* and the *St. Petersburg News*.

1848 Publication of *A Strange Wife, A Faint Heart,* "The Stories of a Veteran," *The Christmas Tree and the Wedding, White Nights, The Jealous Husband,* and *The Landlady,* all in *Notes from the Fatherland*. The latter work draws harsh criticism from Belinsky.

1849	Dostoevsky arrested for his role in the Petrashevsky circle, and imprisoned in St. Petersburg's Peter and Paul Fortress. Sentenced to death, but at the last minute the sentence is commuted to four years of forced labor in Siberia. Sent to Omsk, where he remains until 1854.
1854	Dostoevsky enlists in the army as a private and is sent to Semipalatinsk, near the Mongolian border.
1856	Promoted to lieutenant.
1857	Marries Maria Dmitrievna Isaeva, a widow. *A Little Hero* published anonymously in *Notes from the Fatherland.*
1858	Released from army; leaves Semipalatinsk for Tver.
1859	Is permitted to return to St. Petersburg. "Uncle's Dream" published in *The Russian Word; A Friend of the Family* published in *Notes from the Fatherland.*
1860	Introduction and first chapter to *Notes from the House of the Dead* are published. Work meets opposition from the censor at *The Russian Word.*
1861	*Notes from the House of the Dead* in its entirety and *The Insulted and the Injured* are published in *Time,* a journal recently started by Dostoevsky's brother Mikhail.
1862	First trip abroad. "An Unpleasant Predicament" published in *Time.*
1863	*Winter Notes on Summer Impressions* published in *Time. Time* is suppressed. Second trip abroad.
1864	Publishes magazine, *Epoch,* with brother Mikhail. *Notes from Underground* published in *Epoch.* Death of Dostoevsky's wife, and, within a few months, his brother.
1865	*Epoch* ceases publication. Third trip abroad.
1866	*Crime and Punishment* serialized in *The Russian Herald.* Anna Grigorievna Snitkina comes to work for Dostoevsky as a stenographer. *The Gambler* published.
1867	Marries Snitkina. The couple goes abroad to live for the next four years.
1868	*The Idiot* serialized in *The Russian Herald.* A daughter, Sofia, is born, but dies two months later.
1869	Daughter Lyubov' born in Dresden.
1870	*The Eternal Husband* published in *Dawn.*
1871–72	Returns to St. Petersburg. Son Fyodor born. *The Possessed* serialized in *The Russian Herald.*
1873–74	Editor of *The Citizen. Diary of a Writer* begins publication.

1875	Son Alexey (Alyosha) born. *A Raw Youth* serialized in *Notes from the Fatherland*.
1876	"A Gentle Spirit" published in *Diary of a Writer*.
1877	"Dream of a Ridiculous Man" published in *Diary of a Writer*.
1878	Death of son Alyosha. Dostoevsky visits Optina monastery with Vladimir Solov'yov; they meet Starets Amvrozy.
1879–80	*The Brothers Karamazov* serialized in *The Russian Herald*.
1881	Dostoevsky dies on January 28.

Contributors

HAROLD BLOOM, Sterling Professor of the Humanities at Yale University, is the author of *The Anxiety of Influence, Poetry and Repression,* and many other volumes of literary criticism. His forthcoming study, *Freud: Transference and Authority,* attempts a full-scale reading of all of Freud's major writings. A MacArthur Prize Fellow, he is general editor of five series of literary criticism published by Chelsea House. During 1987–88, he served as Charles Eliot Norton Professor of Poetry at Harvard University.

ALFRED L. BEM, a Russian scholar and critic, emigrated to Prague following the Bolshevik revolution. He wrote widely on Dostoevsky, Pushkin, and others before his disappearance in 1945.

EDWARD WASIOLEK is Professor of Russian and Comparative Literature at The University of Chicago. He is the author of *Dostoevsky: The Major Fiction.*

MICHAEL HOLQUIST has taught Russian literature at the University of Texas at Austin, Indiana University, and Yale University.

A. D. NUTTALL is Professor of English at the University of Sussex and the author of *A Common Sky,* Crime and Punishment: *Murder as a Philosophic Experiment,* and *A New Mimesis.*

ROBERT LOUIS JACKSON is Professor of Russian Literature at Yale University. He is the author of several works on Dostoevsky and has edited a reader on Russian formalism.

DEREK OFFORD is the author of numerous articles on world literature.

JOHN JONES is Professor of Poetry at the University of Oxford and the author of books on Wordsworth, Keats, Dostoevsky, and others.

MIKHAIL BAKHTIN, Russian scholar and literary theorist, is the author of influential studies of Rabelais and Dostoevsky.

145

Bibliography

Adams, Barbara Block. "Sisters under Their Skins: The Women in the Lives of Raskolnikov and Razumov." *Conradiana* 6 (1974): 113–24.

Anderson, Roger B. "*Crime and Punishment:* Psychomyth and the Making of a Hero." *Canadian-American Slavic Studies* 11, no. 4 (Winter 1977): 523–28.

———. "Raskolnikov and Myth Experience." *Slavic and East European Journal* 20 (1976): 1–17.

Bakhtin, Mikhail. *Problems of Dostoevsky's Poetics.* Translated by R. W. Rostel. Ann Arbor, Mich.: Ardis, 1973.

Bayley, John. "Character and Consciousness." *New Literary History* 5 (1974): 234–35.

Bethea, David M. "Structure versus Symmetry in *Crime and Punishment.*" In *Fearful Symmetry: Doubles and Doubling in Literature and Film,* edited by Eugene J. Cook, 41–64. Tallahassee: University Presses of Florida, 1981.

Beyer, Thomas R., Jr. "*Crime and Punishment.*" *The Explicator* 41, no. 1 (Fall 1982): 33–35.

Blodgett, Harriet. "Dostoevsky's *Crime and Punishment.*" The Explicator 40, no. 1 (Fall 1985): 35–37.

Brody, Ervin C. "Meaning and Symbolism in the Names of Dostoevsky's *Crime and Punishment* and *The Idiot.*" *Names* 27, no. 2 (June 1979): 117–40.

Busch, Robert L. "Humor in Dostoevsky's *Crime and Punishment.*" *Canadian-American Slavic Studies* 9, no. 1 (Spring 1975): 54–68.

Cassedy, Steven. "The Formal Problem of the Epilogue in *Crime and Punishment:* The Logic of Tragic and Christian Structures." *Dostoevsky Studies* 3 (1982): 171–89.

Chapple, Richard. "Character Parallels in *Crime and Punishment* and *Sanctuary.*" *Germano-Slavica* 2, no. 1 (Spring 1976): 5–14.

Davydov, Sergei. "Dostoevsky and Nabokov: The Morality of Structure in *Crime and Punishment* and *Despair.*" *Dostoevsky Studies* 3 (1982): 157–70.

Gill, Richard. "The Bridges of St. Petersburg: A Motif in *Crime and Punishment.*" *Dostoevsky Studies* 3 (1982): 145–55.

Goldstein, David I. *Dostoevsky and the Jews.* Austin: University of Texas Press, 1981.

Hart, Pierre. "Looking over Raskolnikov's Shoulder: The Narrator in *Crime and Punishment.*" *Criticism* 13 (1971): 166–79.

147

Holquist, Michael. *Dostoevsky and the Novel*. Princeton: Princeton University Press, 1977.

Horsman, Dorothea. "*Crime and Punishment:* A Study in Technique." *New Zealand Slavonic Journal* 6 (1970): 34–52.

Jones, John. *Dostoevsky*. Oxford: Clarendon Press, 1983.

Jones, Malcolm V. "Raskolnikov's Humanitarianism." *Canadian-American Slavic Studies* 8, no. 3 (Fall 1974): 370–80.

Karyakin, Yuri. *Rereading Dostoevsky*. Translated by S. Chulaki. Moscow: Novosti Press, 1971.

Kiremidjian, David. "*Crime and Punishment*: Matricide and the Woman Question." *The American Imago* 33, no. 4 (Winter 1976): 403–33.

Kreyling, Michael. "*Crime and Punishment:* The Pattern Beneath the Surface of Percy's *Lancelot*." *Notes on Mississippi Writers* 11, no. 1 (Spring 1978): 36–44.

Leatherbarrow, W. J. "Raskolnikov and the 'Enigma of Personality.' " *Forum for Modern Language Studies* 9, no. 2 (April 1973): 153–65.

Leighton, Lauren G. "The Crime and Punishment of Monstrous Coincidence." *Mosaic* 12, no. 1 (Fall 1978): 93–106.

Mann, Robert, "Elijah the Prophet in *Crime and Punishment*." *Canadian Slavonic Papers* 23, no. 3 (September 1981): 261–72.

Naumann, Marina T. "Raskolnikov's Shadow: Porfirij Petrovic." *Slavic and East European Journal* 13 (1971): 166–79.

Pachmuss, Temira. "Dostoevsky's Porfiry Petrovich: A New Socrates." *New Zealand Slavonic Journal* 1 (1980): 17–24.

Rosenshield, Gary. "First- versus Third-Person Narrative in *Crime and Punishment*." *Slavic and East European Journal* 17 (1973): 399–407.

Rowe, W. W. "*Crime and Punishment* and *The Brothers Karamazov:* Some Comparative Observations." *Russian Literature Triquarterly*, no. 10 (1974): 331–42.

———. "Dostoevskian Patterned Antinomy and its Function in *Crime and Punishment*." *Slavic and East European Journal* 16 (1972): 287–96.

Santangelo, Gennaro. "The Five Motives of Raskolnikov." *Dalhousie Review* 54 (Winter 1974–75): 710–19.

Seduro, Vladimir. *Dostoevsky in Russian Literary Criticism 1846–1956*. New York: Octagon, 1969.

Seeley, Frank Friedberg. "The Two Faces of Svidrigailov." *Canadian-American Slavic Studies* 12, no. 3 (Fall 1978): 413–17.

Shaw, J. Thomas. "Raskolnikov's Dreams." *Slavic and East European Journal* 2 (1973): 131–45.

Snodgrass, W. D. "*Crime and Punishment*: The Tenor of Part One." *The Hudson Review* 13 (1960): 202–53.

Wasiolek, Edward. *Dostoevsky: The Major Fiction*. Cambridge, Mass.: MIT Press, 1964.

———, ed. Crime and Punishment *and the Critics*. San Francisco: Wadsworth, 1960.

Welch, Lois M. "Luzhin's Crime and the Advantages of Melodrama in Dostoevsky's *Crime and Punishment*." *Texas Studies in Literature and Language* 18 (1976): 135–46.

Wellek, René. *Dostoevsky: A Collection of Critical Essays*. Englewood Cliffs, N.J.: Prentice-Hall, 1962.

Wilson, Raymond J. "Raskolnikov's Dream in *Crime and Punishment*." *Literature and Psychology* 3 (1976): 159–66.

Zdanys, Jonas. "Raskolnikov and Frankenstein: The Deadly Search for a Rational Paradise." *Cithara* 1 (1976): 57–67.

Acknowledgments

"The Problem of Guilt" by Alfred L. Bem from *Twentieth Century Interpretations of Crime and Punishment*, edited by Robert Louis Jackson, © 1974 by Prentice-Hall, Inc. Reprinted by permission of Prentice-Hall, Inc., Englewood Cliffs, New Jersey.

"Raskolnikov's Motives: Love and Murder" by Edward Wasiolek from *American Imago* 31, no. 3 (Fall 1974), © 1974 by the Association for Applied Psycho-analysis, Inc. Reprinted by permission.

"Puzzle and Mystery, the Narrative Poles of Knowing: *Crime and Punishment*" by Michael Holquist from *Dostoevsky and the Novel* by Michael Holquist, © 1977 by Princeton University Press. Reprinted by permission of Princeton University Press.

"*Crime and Punishment*: Christianity and Existentialism" (originally entitled "The Intellectual Problem: II") by A. D. Nuttall from *Crime and Punishment: Murder as Philosophic Experiment* by A. D. Nutall, © 1978 by A. D. Nuttall. Reprinted by permission.

"Philosophical Pro and Contra in Part 1 of *Crime and Punishment*" by Robert Louis Jackson from *The Art of Dostoevsky: Deliriums and Nocturnes* by Robert Louis Jackson, © 1981 by Princeton University Press. Reprinted by permission of Princeton University Press.

"The Causes of Crime and the Meaning of Law: *Crime and Punishment* and Contemporary Radical Thought" by Derek Offord from *New Essays on Dostoevsky*, edited by Malcolm V. Jones and Garth M. Terry, © 1983 by Cambridge University Press. Reprinted by permission of Cambridge University Press.

"*Crime and Punishment*: Theory and Life" (originally entitled "*Crime and Punishment*" by John Jones from *Dostoevsky* by John Jones, © 1983 by John Jones. Reprinted by permission of Oxford University Press.

"Carnival and Space in *Crime and Punishment*" (originally entitled "Characteristics of Genre") by Mikhail Bakhtin from *Problems of Dostoevsky's Poetics*, edited and translated by Caryl Emerson, © 1984 by the University of Minnesota. Reprinted by permission of the University of Minnesota Press.

151

Index

Library I M C
Champaign Centennial High School
Champaign, Illinois

DISCARD

891.73   29.95
BLOOM
Bloom, Harold Modern Critical
Interpretations: Fyodor Dostoevsk
Crime and Punishment